HERAKLEION
ARCHAEOLOGICAL
MUSEUM

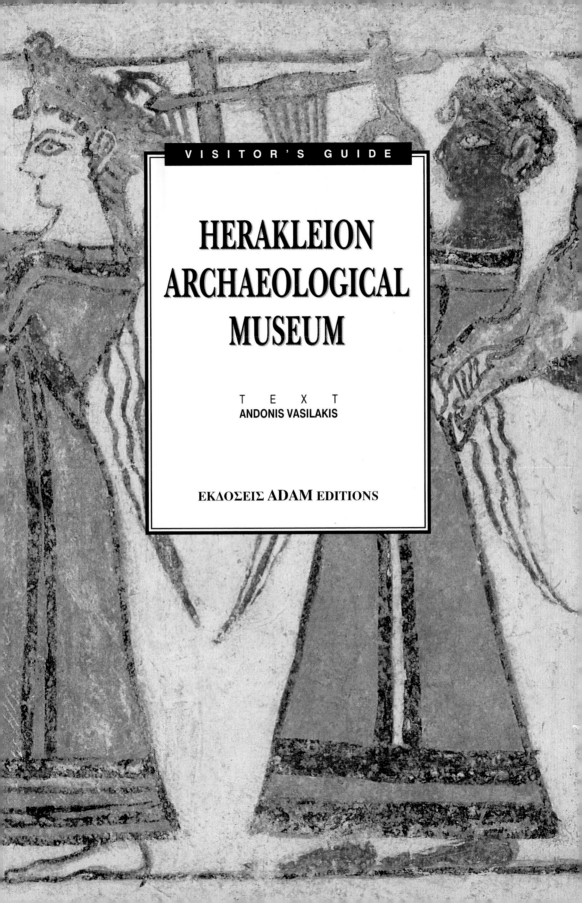

VISITOR'S GUIDE

HERAKLEION ARCHAEOLOGICAL MUSEUM

TEXT
ANDONIS VASILAKIS

ΕΚΔΟΣΕΙΣ **ADAM** EDITIONS

C O N T E N T S

PROLOGUE

p. 8

**PLANS OF
THE GROUND FLOOR AND
FIRST FLOOR**

THE MOST IMPORTANT EXHIBITS
BY ROOM

p. 10

INTRODUCTION

BRIEF HISTORY OF THE CIVILISATION
OF ANCIENT CRETE

p. 12

ROOM I

NEOLITHIC PERIOD (7000-3500 BC)
PRE-PALACE PERIOD (3500-1900 BC)

p. 42

ROOM II

OLD PALACE PERIOD (1900-1700 BC)

p. 58

ROOM III

OLD PALACE PERIOD
THE PALACE AT PHAISTOS

p. 66

ROOM IV

NEW PALACE PERIOD
THE PALACES AT KNOSSOS, PHAISTOS & MALIA

p. 78

ROOM V

MATURE & FINAL PHASES OF THE PALACE
AT KNOSSOS (1450-1300 BC)

p. 92

ROOM VI

THE CEMETERIES AT KNOSSOS, PHAISTOS & ARCHANES

p. 104

ROOM VII

THE PALACE AT AYIA TRIADA
THE MEGARA AT VATHYPETRO, NIROU CHANI, TYLISSOS
& AMNISOS
THE CAVES AT ARKALOCHORI, PSYCHRO & PATSOS
THE CEMETERIES AT MALIA, MOCHLOS, GOURNIA & EPISKOPI

p. 118

ROOM VIII

THE PALACE AT ZAKROS

p. 132

ROOM IX

THE NEW PALACE PERIOD IN EAST CRETE
PALAIKASTRO, PSEIRA, GOURNIA, PISKOKEPHALO,
MOCHLOS & MYRTOS

p. 142

ROOM X
POST-PALACE PERIOD (1400-1100 BC)

p. 152

ROOM XI
SUB-MINOAN, PROTOGEOMETRIC & EARLY
GEOMETRIC PERIODS (1100- 800 BC)

p. 160

ROOM XII
MATURE GEOMETRIC & ORIENTALISING PERIODS
(800-650 BC)

p. 168

ROOM XIII
MINOAN SARCOPHAGI

p. 178

ROOM XIV
MINOAN WALL-PAINTINGS

p. 184

ROOM XV
MINOAN WALL-PAINTINGS

p. 198

ROOM XVI
MINOAN WALL-PAINTINGS

p. 202

ROOM XVII
GIAMALAKIS COLLECTION

p. 208

ROOM XVIII
MINOR ARTS OF ARCHAIC, CLASSICAL, HELLENISTIC &
ROMAN TIMES (7th c. BC - 4th c. AD)

p. 214

ROOM XIX
MONUMENTAL ART OF THE ARCHAIC PERIOD

p. 222

ROOM XX
CLASSICAL, HELLENISTIC & GRECO-ROMAN SCULPTURE

p. 230

EPILOGUE
p. 242

GLOSSARY
p. 244

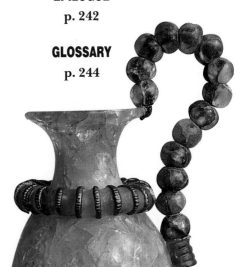

Heraklion Archaeological Museum is both the second largest and second most important museum in Greece, and one of the most important in the world. From the time of its foundation the purpose of the museum has been to house and promote the monuments of the civilisation that flourished on the great island of Minos, without break, from remote pre-history in the seventh millennium BC to the end of the ancient world in the 4th c. AD. Without question the most important groups of exhibits in the museum are the peerless master-pieces created by the Minoan civilisation, the first civilisation in Europe and Greece, which for about twenty centuries domi-nated the Greek and Aegean world. The monuments from the centuries following the end of the Minoan civilisation are no less important, however; this was the period during which Crete played an active role in the creation of Greek Classical civilisation.

Down to the 1960s the Herakleion Museum housed and displayed antiquities from almost the whole of Crete, though mainly from the central and east part of the island. During this and the following decades, new archaeological museums were founded in Ayios Nikolaos, Siteia, Chania and Rethymnon, which now house and display the monuments of Cretan civilisation from sites in east and west Crete.

The present guide offers all visitors to the Herakleion Museum the opportunity to acquire authoritative information on the civilisation of Crete, through monuments covering approximately 8,000 years. It is increasingly necessary in modern times to be acquainted with the immortal creations of the glorious past; works bequeathed to us by men who lived and created on the earth on which we now tread and have our being.

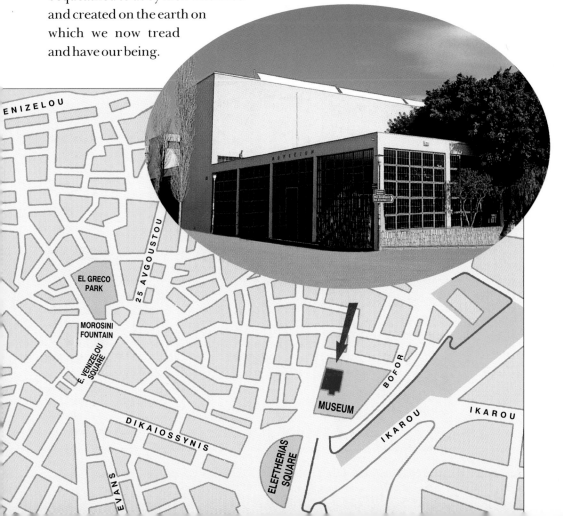

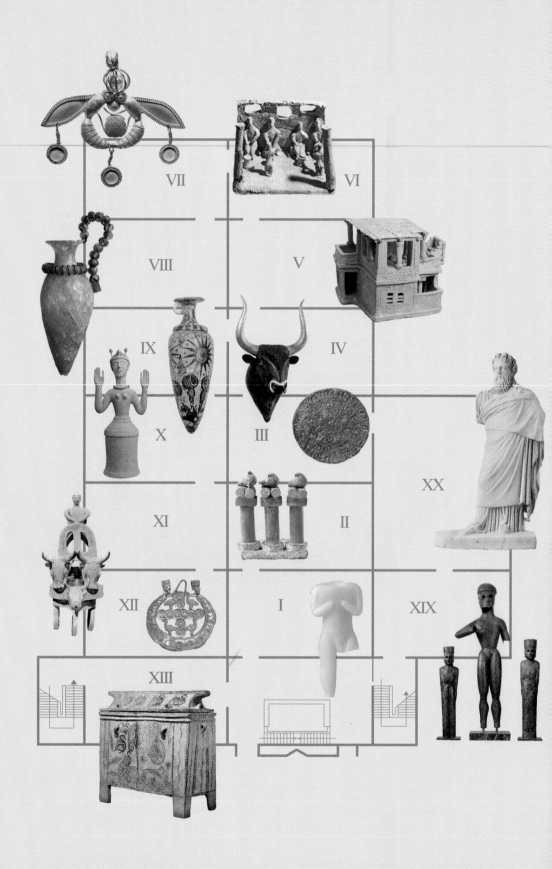

PLANS OF THE
GROUND FLOOR & FIRST FLOOR

THE MOST IMPORTANT EXHIBITS
BY ROOM

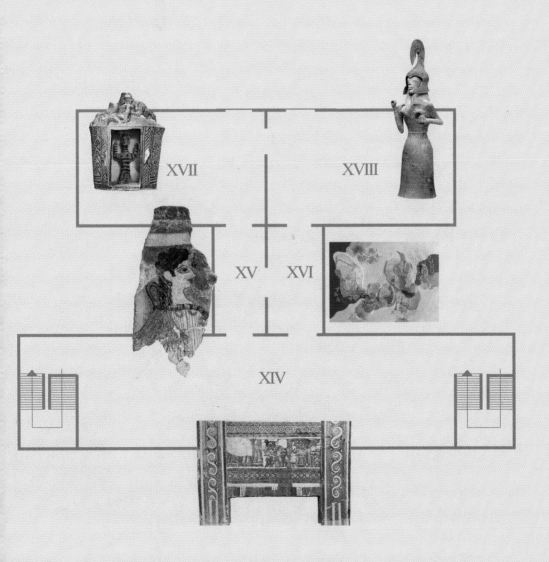

XVII

XVIII

XV XVI

XIV

BRIEF HISTORY
OF THE CIVILISATION
OF ANCIENT CRETE

Scholarly investigation has demonstrated that the history of ancient Crete reaches back over a period of at least eight thousand years. There is some indication that Crete was inhabited even before the Neolithic period, though the evidence is not convincing enough to assert this with any certainty. What is certain is that the island was inhabited from at least as early as the middle of the seventh millennium.

Koumasa:
circular Minoan tomb.
2800-1900 BC.

CRETE FROM THE 7th TO THE 4th MILLENNIUM BC

The Neolithic period

In the Neolithic period (6500-3300 BC), the inhabitants of Crete lived permanently in settlements (at Knossos, Phaistos, Gortyn, Katsambas near Herakleion and elsewhere), in houses with one or two rooms, made of stone, mud and wood. They also dwelt seasonally in caves (Platyvola Chanion, Yerani Rethymnou, Stravomytis on Mount Juktas, the cave of Eileithyia near Amnisos, Miamous, Trapeza Lasithiou, Pelekita Zakrou and others).

They cultivated the soil and engaged in stock-breeding, hunting, fishing and fruit-gathering. Their tools were made of worked stone, wood, bone, horn and obsidian, which they brought from Milos and Nisyros. They made vases of clay for their daily needs. In the beginning these had thick walls and were badly fired, but the technique

Vasiliki:
the "Red House".
2800-2300 BC.

rapidly improved: the surfaces were smoothed and glazed with a brown or greyish-black colour, and in some cases were decorated with incisions. These vases mainly had open shapes, with closed shapes being much rarer. The inhabitants of Neolithic Crete modelled figures of men and animals in clay or carved them in stone. Amongst the best-known of these are the terracotta figurine of a female figure from Ierapetra (Giamalakis Collection) and a marble male figurine from Knossos.

Although relations are attested with the islands of the southern Aegean, Crete gives the impression of being introspective and relatively isolated from the rest of the Aegean world. Nevertheless the population had increased by the fourth millennium and all parts of Crete were inhabited.

The objects dating from the Neolithic period are exhibited in cases 1 and 2 in room I of the museum.

Lebena, Yerokambos: circular Minoan tomb. 3300-1900 BC.

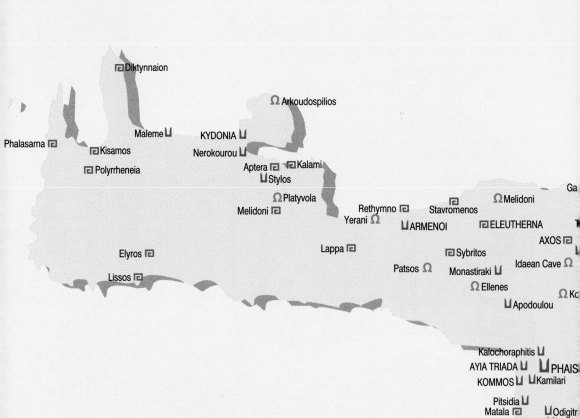

Diktynnaion

Ω Arkoudospilios

Maleme

KYDONIA

Phalasarna   Kisamos   Nerokourou

Polyrrheneia

Aptera   Kalami

Stylos

Ω Platyvola

Melidoni

Ω Melidoni

Ga

Rethymno   Stavromenos

Yerani Ω   ARMENOI   ELEUTHERNA

Elyros   Lappa   Sybritos   AXOS

Lissos   Patsos Ω   Monastiraki   Idaean Cave Ω

Ω Ellenes   Ω Ko

Apodoulou

Kalochoraphitis

AYIA TRIADA   PHAIS

KOMMOS   Kamilari

Pitsidia

Matala   Odigitr

Lassaia   L

THE MOST IMPORTANT ARCHAEOLOGICAL SITES

- ⊔ SITES OF THE MINOAN PERIOD
- ⊡ SITES OF GRECO-ROMAN TIMES
- Ω ARCHAEOLOGICAL CAVES

CRETE

Dia

Ayia Pelayia

Herakleion
Amnnisos   Gournes
Katsambas   Nirou   Chersonisos
okambos   Skotino   Milatos
KNOSSOS   MALIA
Kalo Chorio   Dreros   Elounda
RCHANES   Karphi
              LYKTOS   Trapeza   PSEIRA   Siteia   Ayia Photia   Itanos
Lykastos Juktas   MOCHLOS   PETRAS   PALAIKASTRO
        GALATAS   Plati   Petsophas
RINIAS
Arkalochori   Diktaean Cave   Lato   Maronia   Traostalos
              Vrokastro   Kavousi   ZAKROS
        Arkades   GOURNIA Pachyammos   Praisos
RTYN   Rotasi   Symi   Malles   Pelekita
esokari   Viannos   VASILIKI
oumasa   Makriyalos   Ambelos
os   Cave of Eileithyia/Inatos   Myrtos (Ryrgos)   IERAPETRA
Kophinas   (Tsoutsouros)
Trypiti   Kouphonisi
AS)

CRETE IN THE BRONZE AGE

The Pre-palace period (3300-1900 BC)

The Bronze Age, which began about the middle of the 4th millennium BC, is known in Crete as the Minoan period (3300-1100 BC). After a long preparatory period in the 3rd millennium BC, Crete entered upon the most brillant era of its civilisation.

The first phase, down to 1900 BC, has been called the Pre-palace period and represents a smooth evolution from the previous Neolithic era. Some scholars hold the view that peoples from Africa and Asia Minor settled on Crete at the beginning of this new period, but this theory has been challenged in recent decades. On the contrary, everything points to the fact that there was no change in the population of Crete,

The archaeological site of Knossos.

and that what changes there were occurred gradually and in stages over the course of two or three centuries. New features of the civilisation include the systematic use of bronze and precious metals, a technological advance in the manufacture of clay vases, the use of seals and jewellery, and the development of stone-working. The Cretans came into close contact with the inhabitants of the Aegean islands, mainland Greece and Asia Minor. Crete passed through the phase of early urbanisation at the same time as these regions.

The characteristic features of this development are organised settlements, carefully constructed houses with large numbers of rooms, and large circular or rectangular tombs. Burial customs suggest that society was organised by clans. The basic occupations of the inhabitants continued to be farming and stock-breeding. Part of the population did

The archaeological site of Phaistos.

not take part in these activities, however, but specialised in the craft-in-dustrial production of essential goods (clay or stone vases, metal tools, weapons or jewellery, etc.), and there was an increase in the bartering of products and raw materials (e.g. metals) with neighbouring or more distant regions in the East Mediterranean.

Settlements dating from the Pre-palace period have been excavated at sites in east Crete (Myrtos and Vasiliki near Ierapetra) and south Crete (Trypiti), and also other sites in the centre of the island such as Knossos, Ayia Triada and Phaistos. The urban tissue was formed of streets and squares. Houses were built of masonry consisting of stone in the lower courses with brick above, and had large numbers of rooms. The walls and floors were frequently coated with plaster, and in some cases there were built benches, and pillars to support the roof.

The burial buildings dating from this period are impressive. In south-central Crete the predominant form is the large circular tholos tomb (Ayia Triada, Platanos, Koumasa, the Monastery of the Odigitria, Le-

Archanes,
Anemospilia:
the tripartite shrine.

bena), though rectangular tombs are also found (Kephali Odigitrias), while in north-central Crete both types of tomb are common (Archanes). The predominant form of burial building in east Crete is rectangular (Malia, Mochlos, Palaikastro), and there are also rock-cut tombs (Ayia Photia).

Offerings were placed in the tombs along with the dead: clay and stone vases, bronze daggers, jewellery and seals. In this period there was a significant advance in the quality of manufacture of clay vases, with a variety of shapes and decoration. Vases are found with a monochrome black, grey or brown, surface (Pyrgos style), or with a bichrome surface with linear decoration of brown paint on a light background (Ayios Onouphrios and Koumasa styles), and even with polychrome surfaces that are deliberately unevenly fired (Vasiliki style). At the end of this period the predominant decorative style is white paint on a black slip (white style) while other vases have a relief surface.

Craftsmen working in stone made fine vases and vessels and other objects of miniature art: figurines, necklace beads and sealstones.

Bronze tools and weapons, and gold and silver jewellery attest to the systematic practice of metal-working, the new technology of the era, in which bronze, silver and gold were used to make tools and other objects. The goldsmith's art in particular flourished greatly. Superb hair jewellery, necklaces, pendants and other jewellery for the body and clothing have been discovered in tombs dating from the Early Bronze Age.

Soft materials such as ivory, bone and faience were also used to make seals, figurines and jewellery.

The standard of living was quite advanced. Commercial exchanges with the outside world are attested by the importing of raw materials and finished objects. Obsidian and silver was imported from the Cyclades, gold from the north Aegean, bronze from Cyprus and elsewhere, ivory from Syria and tin from Asia Minor.

At the end of this period the Minoans established their first settlement outside Crete, on the island of Kythera. The artefacts dating from Pre-palace Crete are displayed in cases 3 to 18 in room I of the museum.

The Old Palace period (c. 1900-1700 BC)

About 2000-1900 BC the rate of development on Crete became unprecedentedly rapid. The brilliant new era has been called the Old

Malia: view of the
archaeological site.

Palace or the Protopalatial period. The creation of the first palaces at Knossos, Phaistos and Malia led to the cultural unification of Crete in large geographical and political units. The palace centres evolved from the larger settlements of the final centuries of the Pre-palace period.

Around the palaces, and also at other sites, the most dynamic economic communities (Zakros, Kydonia, Monasteraki, Palaikastro, Archanes, Kommos) were amalgamated into urban centres or cities. Life was organised around the palaces. Crete experienced its most brilliant and longest period of prosperity, the Palace period, which lasted for about six or seven centuries (from 2000/1900 to 1400/ 1300 BC).

The first palaces were large and built to a plan which set aside areas for special purposes: residential areas, sanctuaries, storerooms and workshops. Wings of the palaces were repaired during the course of this period. The core of the multi-storey palace, its lungs and light-source, was the main paved courtyard. The materials used in the

Archanes:
the cemetery
at Phourni.

construction of the palaces were stone, wood and mud. The lower part of the walls were faced with slabs of marble, alabaster or gypsum; higher up they were covered with decorative plaster and at the end of the period with wall-paintings.

In the sphere of craft-industries, one particularly advanced sector

Zakros:
the Minoan
palace/harbour
town. 1600-1450 BC.

was that of the organised pottery workshops, particularly in the large palaces at Knossos and Phaistos, where the most brilliant examples of pottery in the polychrome Kamares style, were produced. Vases made in these workshops, and the farm produce of the fertile island of Crete were the main items in the barter trade, which was controlled by the palaces.

The output of clay vases increased significantly at the beginning of this period, when the quick potter's wheel came into use. Stone artefacts made of precious and semiprecious stones also reflect the artistic taste of the period.

The earliest systematic use of writing in Greece is attested in the Old Palace period. It was the Minoans who invented writing in the Aegean. This early script consisted of ideograms and its texts are preserved on sealstones and pieces of clay from the palace archives. The clay tablets contain lists of illustrated objects combined with ideograms and numerals.

Ayia Triada: partial view of the archaeological site.

Terracotta, and more rarely bronze figurines of men, women and animals were produced, which were offered together with other ob-

Diktaean Cave:
a majestic stalactite.
2500-500 BC.

jects as dedications in the sanctuaries where the deity was wor-
shipped, in the palaces, on the peaks of mountains and in caves.
During this period the Minoans founded trading posts - colonies on
Milos, Thera and Kea. Trade was conducted with every area of the
East Mediterranean, Egypt, the coast of Syria and Palestine, and of
course with mainland Greece, the Aegean islands and Asia Minor.
The artefacts from the first palace and cemeteries of Knossos (cases

21, 22, 23, 25, 27, 28, 29), and Malia (cases 19, 25, 26), and also from peak sanctuaries dating from the Old Palace Period (cases 20, 21, 21a, 24, 25) are displayed in room II. The finds from the first palace at Phaistos and from the temple at Anemospilia at Archanes are displayed in room III of the museum.

The New Palace Period (c. 1700-1450 BC)

The first palaces were destroyed by earthquake and fire about 1700 BC. The new period has been called the New Palace Period. The second (or new) palaces were very quickly erected at Knossos, Phaistos and Malia, to roughly the same plan; though slightly smaller in size, they were more brilliant and more carefully constructed. In some cases use was made in them of sections or walls of the first palaces. New large or smaller palaces and palace buildings were erected for the first time at Zakros, Archanes, Ayia Triada, Kommos,

Palaikastro:
the Minoan town.
1600-1200 BC.

Kydonia (Chania), Galata Pediadas, Gournia and Petra Siteias. Large urban centres flourished around the palaces mentioned above, and also at other sites: at Palaikastro, Mochlos, Pseira, Myrtos, Tylissos, Gortyn and Kommos.

Gournia:
the Minoan town.
1600-1200 BC.

Megara, villas and farmhouses were built in the cities and in the countryside: Tylissos, Gortyn, Siteia, Nirou, Amnisos, Vathypetro, Makriyalos, Pitsidia, Pretoria, Nerokourou and Myrtos. The megara and villas were miniature copies of the palaces. Both palaces and megara were decorated with brilliant wall-paintings.

The palaces played a complex role: they were centres of the political authority and of religious life, and also large economic centres with warehouses, workshops and the residences of the "royal family". The role played by the palaces as religious centres is, together with their economic function, perhaps the most important. These two roles, indeed, were interlinked. The storerooms were protected by the deity, since they existed side by side with sanctuaries of various kinds and purposes. The palaces were occupied by the kings or the rulers with their families. They enjoyed some astonishing conveniences, even by modern standards. The palaces were the home of the political authority and had a complex bureaucracy. Economic activity was directed and regulated by the rulers. They collected and recorded the products of the countryside and coordinated trade. Control over economic life was secured through a system of recording the output, which was produced and collected in the palace for storage and redistribution, and also of the raw materials and products of the workshops. The recording, storage and control of produce is attested also by the large number of clay sealings and incised texts in the ideogrammatic script and also in Linear A, which was in use at this period.

Religious worship took place, as during the previous period, in sanctuaries outside the settlements (caves and peak sanctuaries), though mainly in palace and domestic shrines in the palaces and megara. Various religious ceremonies and festivals were held in the courtyards of the palaces, including bull-leaping and sacred dances. The palaces and megara were decorated with brilliant wall-paintings, which have unfortunately survived only in fragments, displayed with much restoration and supplementation in rooms XIV, XV and XVI of the museum. The dead were buried in rock-cut tombs or in

Myrtos, Pyrgos: the courtyard and megaron. 1600-1450 BC.

Tylissos:
general view of the
Minoan megara.
1600-1200 BC.

sarcophagi and pithoi placed in built square or rectangular tombs. The arts prospered greatly. Pottery was dominated by two new decorative bichrome styles: the floral and marine styles. The decoration was executed in dark (ranging from light red to dark brownish-black) paint on the light ground of the vase. In the floral style, which is slightly earlier, floral motifs were used: rosettes and other flowers, leaves, tendrils and branches, frequently combined with other motifs, mainly religious symbols (axes, helmets, sacral knots), bands, chequer-board pattern, etc. The marine style derives its decorative motifs from the world of the sea: octopuses, cuttlefish, nautilus argonauts, starfish, shells, and rocks by the coast adorn the vases in this style, which are usually in the shape of conical or ovoid rhyta.

In the sphere of stone-working, the palace workshops produced fine objects worked in various stones. The most important of them, rhyta and other vases and vessels, come from the palaces at Knossos, Zakros and Ayia Triada.

Bronze was used to make a large number of tools, weapons and vessels. The goldsmith's art reached a pinnacle with the creation of gold jewellery. Finger-rings, necklaces, pins, amulets and earrings come from the royal cemeteries at Knossos, Archanes, Malia, Phaistos and Ayia Triada.

Seals were now made of hard precious and semiprecious stones. Signet-rings were made of precious metals, gold and silver. Small-scale sculpture in clay, metal, rock, ivory and glass paste produced figurines, jewellery and other small *objets d'art*.

Crete cultivated strong foreign relations. The economic and cultural influence of the island on mainland Greece and the islands was decisive for the future history of these areas. Some cities and islands were Minoanised to a high degree and became true major urban centres in which wealth was accumulated; they include Thera, Milos, Kea, Aegina, Kythera, Rhodes, Miletos (perhaps the largest Minoan colony of this period) and Cyprus.

Pseira: the Minoan harbour settlement. 1700-1450 BC.

The island also enjoyed close relations with other regions in the East Mediterranean (Egypt, Asia Minor and Syria-Palestine). These rela-

Palaikastro: large Minoan house. 1700-1450 BC.

Vathypetro: the large Minoan villa/megaron. 1600-1500 BC.

tions are attested by objects from these regions found in Crete and
vice versa.

The finds from the second palaces, the megara, the settlements, the
cemeteries and the sanctuaries are displayed in rooms IV, V, VI,
VII, VIII, IX, XIII, XIV, XV, XVI and XVII.

The Post-palace Period (c. 1450-1100 BC)

About 1450/30 BC, the brilliant civilisation of the second palaces was
delivered a severe blow by a natural disaster, a fire that was possibly
the result of an enemy invasion from mainland Greece. The palaces
were razed to the ground, apart from that at Knossos. It was not a
decisive blow, however. Until a few years ago it was believed that the
cause of the disaster was the major eruption of the Thera volcano
and its consequences. It is now believed by almost all scholars that
the eruption of the volcano took place about 150-200 years earlier
than the fall of the Minoan palaces (1620/1600 BC).

After the middle of the 15th c. BC, Crete followed a different course.
It was no longer the main centre of cultural influence in the Aegean
world. This role had now passed to the centres in mainland Greece
(Mycenae, Pylos, Thebes and elsewhere). Nevertheless, Knossos was
one of the five strongest Mycenaean kingdoms, along with Mycenae,
Pylos, Thebes and Iolkos.

The new period, from 1450 to 1100 BC, is normally known as the Post-palace period for the whole of Crete (it is so called in the signs in Herakleion Museum and in most of the books in print). In the case of the area of Knossos (the palace town, the harbour town at Katsambas and Poros near Herakleion) a brief period (normally 50-70 years) is recognised as an 'advanced and final phase of the New-Palace civilisation' (down to 1380/75 BC). Another name for this brief period is 'the Mycenaean phase of the palace at Knossos', while in the case of the Old-Palace cities, the period 1380-1100 BC is still known today, rather infelicitously, as the 'reoccupation period'.

Recent studies of the old finds from Knossos, and important new excavations at other centres in Crete (Ayia Triada, Kommos, Kydonia) give a distinctly different picture from the one hitherto prevailing. Knossos retained its role as the capital of the entire island. The third palace, which was the product of a remodelling of the previous (second) one, appears to have survived until at least 1300 BC, when it too was finally destroyed, probably as the result of an enemy invasion

Kamilari, near Phaistos: the tholos tomb. 1900-1300 BC.

Amnisos:
the villa of the lilies.
1600-1500 BC.

from the Greek mainland. According to some very recent and very bold views, the interval from 1450 to 1300 BC may be called the Third Palace Period.

The civilisation of Crete was influenced by Mycenaean civilisation. The influences reside in the prevailing military-martial spirit, as shown by the weapons in the tombs, the predominance of chamber tombs similar to those in mainland Greece, the forms and decoration of pottery and metal vases, and the style of the wall-paintings.

The most important cultural change was the use of the Minoan Linear B Script, which was used to write texts of an economic content in a Greek-Mycenaean language, initially at the palace at Knossos, approximately one and a half centuries before similar texts were being written in mainland Greece.

Notable palace buildings were erected at Ayia Triada, which became the headquarters of the kingdom of Mesara, and at the harbour-town of Kommos, in the bay of Mesara. Even more important are the indications of the existence of a palace at this period in Kydonia (Chania) in west Crete, where there has been an interesting discovery of Linear B tablets. These centres flourished until 1250 or 1200 BC. The finds from the Post-palace period from palaces, settlements, sanctuaries and cemeteries are displayed in some of the cases in rooms V, VI, VII and in all the cases in room X.

The Sub-minoan Period

At the end of the 13th century Crete followed the fortunes of the rest of the Greek world and went into decline. Some marked cultural changes are nevertheless observable about 1100 BC. The brief period 1100-1050 BC has been called Sub-minoan and is considered a transitional period from the Bronze Age to the Iron Age. During this period the old large centres continued to be inhabited, and at the same time new settlements were founded on high, inaccessible sites, a circumstance thought to indicate insecurity: the preconditions needed for continuous peace in Crete and Greece in general had now vanished.

Prinias:
temple A. 700-550 BC.

CRETE IN THE FIRST MILLENNIUM BC

The Protogeometric period to Hellenistic times (c. 1000-67 BC)

The major upheavals that took place in Crete in the final two centuries of the second millennium continued into the first two centuries of the first. From this transitional phase emerged a new form
political organisation in Crete – independent city-states which, for
centuries, when they were not fighting each other, were entering into alliances with one another against the rest. The political and cultural homogeneity of the Minoan Palace period was a thing of the
past. Its place was taken by cultural fragmentation and the independent evolution of different regions. The new cities of Crete had an
acropolis with a clearly defensive character, especially from the
eighth century onwards. Phalasarna, Polyrrhenia, Kydonia and
Aptera in west Crete, Lappa, Axos and Eleutherna in the area
around Rethymnon, Gortyn, Phaistos, Rhytion, Arkades, Lyktos
and Rizenia (Prinias) in central Crete, and Dreros, Lato and Praisos
in east Crete, are all typical examples of these acropoleis.

The exception was Knossos, which was never fortified. The city
extended over the region to the north, west and north-west of the
ruined palace, on which all that stood was the temple of Rhea,
while its cemetery was even further to the north. A temple in honour of Rhea was also built to the south of the palace of Phaistos.
The building of sanctuaries on the ruins of the Minoan palaces and
other Minoan centres, such as on the palatial harbour-town of
Kommos, points to some continuity in religion from the previous
period.

On other sites, too, where there had been a strong Minoan presence
in the past, human activity continued in one way or another. One
such site is the acropolis of Gortyn, where the settlement of the final
Minoan phase gave way to a Geometric settlement and a Geometric-
Archaic sanctuary of Athena Polias, with some excellent sculptural
architectural decoration. At Prinias (ancient Rizenia), a new settlement dating from Geometric and Archaic times was built on the site
of the Late Minoan settlement, with some temples of importance for
their sculptural architectural decoration.

Another important site is the sanctuary at Symi Viannou; here a
sanctuary dating from the first millennium BC and dedicated to

Hermes and Aphrodite continued to function above the Minoan peak sanctuary.

The mountain settlement-refuge at Karphi on Mount Dikte was founded about 1200 BC on the site of an earlier Minoan peak sanctuary, and continued to function until 800 BC, when it was abandoned. Mountain settlements similar to that at Karphi have been discovered at Gria Vigla in south Crete, at Kavousi, and at Vrokastro on the bay of Mirabellou.

Many caves also continued to be used as cult areas from the Minoan period down to late antiquity. Typical examples are the Idaean and Diktaean Caves, the cave of Eileithyia Inatos at Tsoutsouros in south Crete, and those of Hermes Kranaios at Patsos Amariou and Meldonios at Rethymnon.

Karphi:
the Minoan settlement. 1300-1000 BC.

Symi:
the sacred mountain
(Hermes and Aphrodite).
2000 BC - AD 500.

In the eighth century the first cities were organised at Dreros and
Lato, with their agora and temples. Large temples and public buildings (an ekklesiasterion or assembly building, into which the famous
law code was built), were erected at Gortyn. Because of continuous
occupation and frequent earthquakes, very few remains have survived from the first millennium BC in most of the cities. The man-
made harbour at Phalasarna dating from the Classical period is impressive. The Cretans were pirates and mercenaries down to the Roman conquest. Cretan mercenaries distinguished themselves as warriors. Alexander the Great's admiral, Nearchos, came from Lato.
In the Archaic (7th and 6th c. BC) and particularly in the Classical
period (5th and 4th c. BC), the Cretan cities remained on the mar-
gins of the political developments that determined the history of the

Gortyn:
partial view of the
archaeological side.

Greek world. They were not culturally isolated, however. The law code of Sparta was traditionally derived from Crete. The great philosophers Plato and Aristotle sang the praises of the constitution and laws of the Cretan cities, which, of course, were conservative and strict. The Cretan myths exercised a particular fascination for the rest of the Greeks. Poets, musicians and philosophers, such as Epimenides and Thales, and artists, such as the sculptors Dipoinos and Skylis, the followers of Daedalos, became famous throughout the entire Greek world. One brilliant phase of Greek sculpture, the Daedalic phase of the 7th c., was created in Crete, where some important works produced by it have survived.

The strategic significance of Crete, which during the two millennia of the Minoan period had made it the greatest centre of civilisation in the Greek world, was appreciated once more in the Hellenistic period by the new powers of the time, the Greek states (the Egypt of the Ptolemies, Pergamon, Macedonia) and, finally, in the first century BC by Rome. The harbours of Crete (Phalasarna, Itanos) controlled the new trade routes between the three continents. The major cities of Crete (Knossos, Gortyn, Lyttos, Kydonia and Ierapetra), when they were not fighting each other, were entering into alliance against the rest. They destroyed each other while at the same uniting in the Cretan League, though relations in this were rather loose. On occasion, too, the Cretan cities entered into alliances with the powerful states of the time. Large public works were erected in all the cities, and have survived at Knossos, Lato, Gortyn, Phaistos, Polyrrhenia, Rizenia, Arkades, Praisos, Eleutherna, Axos and elsewhere.

The artistic activity of the Geometric and Archaic periods (10th to 6th c. BC) is represented in Herakleion Archaeological Museum by clay vases, of which the majority were found in graves in the cemeteries of the great cities at Knossos, Arkades, and others. There are some fine architectural reliefs from the temples at Prinias and Gortyn, statues of kouroi from Eleutherna and Astritsi, stone birds from the sanctuary of Zeus at Amnisos, bronze statues from Dreros, and bronze shields from the Idaean Cave. There is also a large number of works of minor art in bronze, clay, and stone, from the major sanctuaries and cemeteries.

The surviving works of art from the Classical and Hellenistic periods are somewhat fewer. They consist mainly of grave reliefs and metopes from Rethymnon, Knossos, Ayia Pelayia and Gortyn. Typical creations of this period are the works of figurine modelling – small terracotta figurines and relief plaques made in moulds. The ceramic vases exhibit strong Attic influence, while the minor arts and coinage reveal clear Minoan influences. The cities of Crete struck coins as early as about 500 BC, with scenes derived from Cretan myths: Europa with Zeus/Bull or an eagle, the Minotaur, the labyrinth, Apollo with a lyre, Artemis with her deer, Triton, Herakles, Kydon suckled by a dog, Demeter, and enthroned figures (Hera, Zeus, Minos and Persephone).

The finds from the settlements, cities, sanctuaries and cemeteries of the Protogeometric down to the Hellenistic period are displayed in rooms XI, XII, XVIII, XIX

Lebena:
The Asklepieion.
3rd c. BC 3rd c. AD.

CRETE IN LATE ANTIQUITY

Greco-Roman times (67 BC-AD 330)

The monuments of the last four centuries of civilisation in Crete are displayed in Herakleion Museum in rooms XVII and XX. This is the period of the Roman occupation in Crete, which together with the Cyrenaica constituted a Roman province with its capital at Gortyn and was governed by a general with proconsular powers. Knossos, which had taken a lead in the resistance to Rome, was punished and demoted to the status of a Roman colony with the name *Colonia Julia Nobilis Cnosus*. Alongside the military and administrative services of the Roman governor, the cities of Crete formally preserved their administrative independence, their political institutions, (council chamber and annually elected officials) and their loose federation, the Cretan League, which continued to function until the end of the 4th c. AD. The period of Roman rule was for Crete one of prosperity and demographic increase. Piracy was eradicated from her harbours as part of the *pax Romana*. Many of the cities prospered and grew rich, with imposing public buildings, and were adorned by statues of emperors and gods, and architectural reliefs, as well as marble relief sarcophagi. The capital, Gortyn, Kisamos, Kydonia, Phalasarna, Polyrrhenia, Aptera, Lappa, Sybritos, Eleutherna, Axos, Lyktos, Knossos, Chersonisos, Ierapytna and other cities all preserve brilliant ruins dating from this period. The Asklepieia at Lebena and Lissos prospered. Other flourishing sanctuaries include the Diktynaean and the Idaean Caves. The countryside also flourished. Large country villas were rebuilt at many sites 1500 years after the New Palace period. The aqueducts of Lyktos, Chersonisos and Gortyn are notable technical feats of an impressive scale. The output of farming increased to the degree that Crete exported corn to Rome. In the second half of the 1st c. AD, the Christian religion was brought to Crete by the Apostles Paul and Titus, who came to Gortyn.

The Early Byzantine period is presented in the Historical Museum of Crete, which is a continuation of the Archaeological Museum.

NOTE:
The dates in this book do not always agree with these on the signs in the Museum.

C H R O N O L O G I C A L   T A B L E

NEOLITHIC PERIOD (7000-3500 BC)

BRONZE AGE (3500-1000 BC)
Pre-palace period .... (3500-1900 BC)
Old Palace period................................. (1900-1700/1650 BC)
New Palace period .... (1700/1650-1450 BC)
Third Palace period .... (1450-1350/1300 BC)
Post-palace period .... (1350/1300-1100 BC)
Sub-minoan period .... (1100-1000 BC)

EARLY IRON AGE (1000-67 BC)
Protogeometric period .... (1000-800 BC)
Geometric period .... (800-700 BC)
Early Archaic (Orientalising) period .... (700-650 BC)
Mature Archaic period .... (650-500 BC)
Classical period .... (500-330 BC)
Hellenistic period .... (330-67 BC)

GRECO-ROMAN PERIOD (67 BC-AD 323)

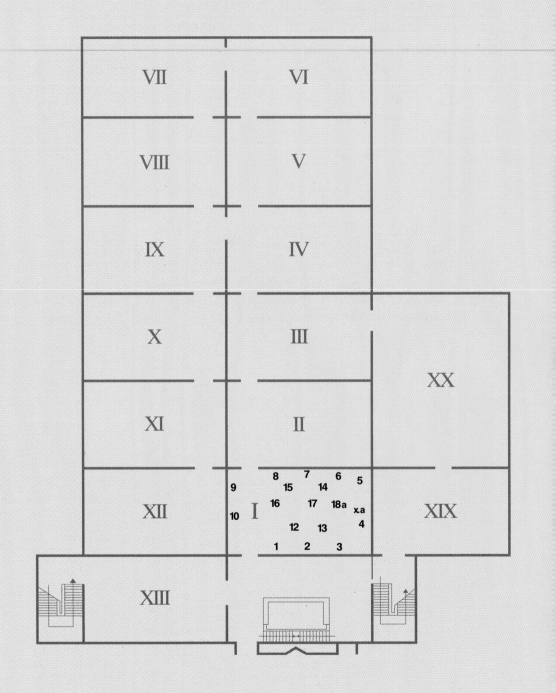

ROOM I

NEOLITHIC PERIOD (7000-3500 B.C.)
PRE-PALACE PERIOD (3500-1900 B.C.)

Stone tools (mattocks) of the Neolithic period.

The exhibits in this room come from the Neolithic settlement at Knossos and the Pre-palace settlements and cemeteries of east Crete (Mochlos, Gournia, Vasiliki, Palaikastro), south-central Crete (Mesara, Asterousia), the south coast (Koumasa, Platanos, Ayia Triada, Lebena), and north-central Crete (Acharnes). They include: Neolithic stone (a single one of marble) and terracotta figurines; very fine examples of Pre-palace clay vases in various styles (the best amongst them are the burnished Pyrgos style vases, the painted Ayios Onouphrios, Koumasa and white style vases, the mottled Vasiliki wares and the earliest example of the barbotine style); clay vessels and figurines; stone vases and figurines; gold and silver jewellery and tools; bronze tools; jewellery of various materials; and seals.

Cylindrical pyxis with incised decoration.
Late Neolithic period.

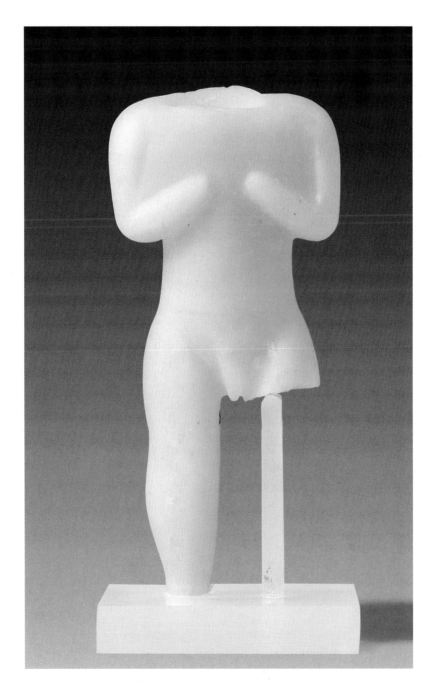

Male figurine of white marble. Early Neolithic period.

Pendent pyxis with lid, in the Ayios Nikolaos style.

Biconical cup (communion chalice) of black fabric with burnished Pyrgos style decoration.

Case 1

Clay vases, parts of clay vases and terracotta figurines of female figures and animals from the Neolithic settlements at **Knossos** and **Katsambas** and from the **Cave of Eileithyia at Amnisos** (6300-3500 BC). The vases have open and closed shapes.

Stone, microlithic, and bone tools from Knossos and other sites.

Case 2

Clay vases from the Neolithic settlements at **Knossos** and **Phaistos** and narrow-necked vases of red fabric, from the well at **Phourni Merambelou** (3500-3300 BC).

Terracotta figurine of a seated male from Knossos.

Terracotta female figurine from Phaistos.

Superb marble male figurine from Knossos.

Case 3

Cups with horn-like protrusions from the Final Neolithic period (3500-3300 BC) and the early Pre-palace period (3300-2900 BC), from **Partera.**

Jug with a globular base with linear, dark on light Ayios Onouphrios style decoration.

Vases made of coloured stone: nest-shaped vase, jug, alabastron, drinking cup.

Jugs and cups of the Ayios Onouphrios style with dark-on-light decoration, from **Ayios Onouphrios near Phaistos** (3300-1900 BC)

Pyrgos style pottery with burnished and incised decoration on a grey or black surface, from the tomb at **Pyrgos near Herakleion** (3300-2900 BC). The shape of the communion chalice is typical. The double and triple cups are called *kernoi*; these were religious vessels used for offering liquid libations or fruit to the deity.

Case 4
Finds from the Pre-palace tholos tomb cemetery at Lebena (3300-1900 BC)

Cups, pyxides (jewellery boxes) and jugs in the Pyrgos, Ayios Onouphrios and Lebena styles (light-on-dark decoration), and with incised decoration. Some of the vases have horn-like protrusions.

Clay models of animals and objects (huts, ships, barrels, fruit, etc.).

In the corner is a large Neolithic clay vase from **Knossos**.

Unnumbered case* between cases 4 and 5

Finds from the cemetery at Phourni, Archanes (2300- 1700 BC)

Cups, jugs, skyphoi, kernoi, baskets from the third Pre-palace (white style) and the Old Palace period (Kamares style).
Clay anthropomorphic vase with two mouths.
Unique clay sistrum.
Burial of a skull in a deep clay vase.

Case 5

Finds from the Pre-palace cemetery at Lebena (3300-1900 BC)

Pottery in the Ayios Onouphrios and Koumasa styles.
Stone vases, marble figurines of Cycladic type, and microlithic tools made of obsidian.

Beak-spouted jug, with mottled Vasiliki style decoration.

* *Some of the cases are not numbered (they are marked on the plans with the initials n.n.) because of changes made to the display some years ago. The order in which they are described is from right to left, ending at the centre. it is possible there will be other changes in the future, and you are requested to find out about them from the signs in the museum.*

Small bronze tongue-shaped and long narrow daggers.
Necklaces of coloured stones and gold beads.
Intact gold diadem.

In the corner is a bathtub-shaped sarcophagus from the tomb
at **Pyrgos**.

Case 6
Finds from the Pre-palace settlements at Vasiliki, Gournia and Mochlos

Oinochoai and "teapots" of the middle Pre-palace period
(2900-2300 BC) in the Vasiliki style. They are decorated with
controlled uneven firing, creating black and red patches.

Jug with a long, beaked spout
and linear white on dark
decoration.

Jug with a long spout and
linear white-style
decoration, with white on dark.

Three-handled jug with relief barbotine decoration.

Terracotta model of a bull with three bull-leapers hanging from its horns.

Case 7
Finds from the Pre-palace cemeteries at Mochlos, Maronia and Zakros (3300-1900 BC)
Stone vases of local soft stone (steatite, limestone, alabaster, conglomerate etc.). The pyxis from Mochlos and the lid of another one from Zakros, of green schist and made by the same craftsman, are masterpieces; they each have a reclining dog in place of the lid handle.
Another important exhibit is the schist vase with a relief spiral from Maronia, which is preserved in two pieces.

Case 8
Finds from the settlements and cemeteries at Vasiliki and Mochlos (2300-1900 BC)
Cups and jugs in the white style (white and more rarely red on a black surface, decorated with spirals, bands and stylised fish).

Clay libation vase in the shape of a female figure with the arms folded across the breast (depiction of the mother goddess).
Head of a small terracotta figurine.
Terracotta model of a sacred ship and double horns.

Case 9
Finds from the Pre-palace cemeteries and tholos tombs in Mesara
Jugs and cups in the barbotine style (2100-1900 BC) with a relief surface and more rarely with added colour.
Bronze basin.

Stone kernos (vase with several cavities), made of schist.

Case 10
Finds from the settlement and tombs at Palaikastro near Siteia (2300-1900 BC)
Cups, small jugs, fruit-stand, and lamps in the white style.
Terracotta models of a ship and a four-wheeled cart.

Low cylindrical pyxis (jewellery box) made of schist, with a reclining dog in place of the handle.

Figurine of a seated figure, of white marble.

Clay cups with animals, birds etc.
Clay votive basin with a model of a shepherd and his flock.

Case 12
Clay jugs, tall conical vase, pyxis and small pithoi in various styles of the Pre-palace period.
Clay libation vase in the shape of a bull with humans on its horns (the earliest depiction of bull-leaping).
Clay libation vases in the form of a woman, a bird etc.

Case 13
Marble figurines of naked female figures of Cycladic (Koumasa) type from the **tombs of Mesara**.
Marble seated figurine of a male figure from **Tekes Knossou.**
Ivory figurines from various sites.
Marble offering-tables and a variety of stone tools.

Case 14
Small bronze daggers with tongue-like and long narrow blades from the **tombs of Mesara.**
Silver daggers from the tombs at **Koumasa, Viannos** and **Tekes Knossou.**
Bronze tool with an ivory handle from the **cave of Trapeza.**
Bronze double axe.
Ivory sword pommels.
Bronze tweezers, blades, scrapers, knives, spits etc.

Case 15
Clay models of animals (rhyta) from the **tombs of Mesara.**
Stone nest-shaped pots and double, triple and quadruple kernoi of soft coloured stones.
Necklaces of coloured stone beads.
Terracotta model of an animal.
Plastic vase in the shape of a bull.

Case 16
Pre-palace seals
Seals made of ivory, steatite and other soft materials in various shapes (prismatic, cylindrical, ring-shaped, zoomorphic) with linear motifs and ideograms on the sealing surfaces. Some are made of silver.
Babylonian cylinder seal of Hamurabi (18th c. BC).
Ivory seal with fourteen sealing surfaces from Phourni, **Archanes**.

Cycladic-type figurine in ivory, imitating a marble figurine.

Gold head ornament consisting of a group of gold leaves, imitating olive leaves.

Case 17

Finds from the Pre-palace cemeteries of Mesara and Mochlos

Gold and a small quantity of silver jewellery from the tombs of Mochlos and Mesara, consisting of ornaments made of gold sheet that were used to adorn the heads, arms and clothing of the dead.

Necklaces of gold and rock-crystal beads.

The small gold frog, the cylindrical bead with attached spirals,

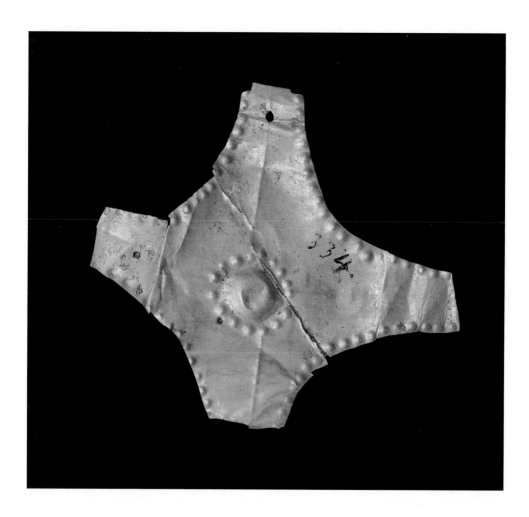

the flower-shaped hairpins, the pendants with delicate chains, and the diadems are all masterpieces of the goldsmith's art.

Gold ornament in the shape of a cross, designed to be sewn to clothing.

Case 18
Finds from Tholos Tomb C at Phourni, Archanes
Marble Cycladic figurine.
Ivory figurine imitating Cycladic marble figurines.
Bronze dagger.
Gold jewellery (necklaces, bands).

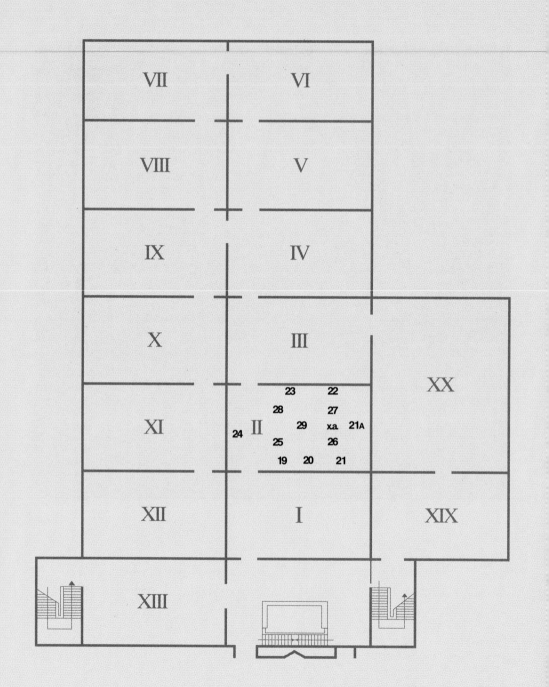

ROOM II

OLD PALACE PERIOD (1900-1700 BC)

The exhibits in this room come from the first palaces, which were built around 2000/1900 BC at Knossos and Malia, and from the peak sanctuaries on Mount Juktas near Archanes, Tylissos, Kalo Chorio Pediadas, Kophinas, Petsophas and Zakros, from the sacred repositeries at Gournia and Tylissos, and from the tombs at Apesokari and Kamilari.

Case 19
From the palace and town of Malia
Pre-palace pottery of various shapes from the deeper levels, beneath the palace at Malia.
Jugs in the Vasiliki style and jugs decorated with relief rosettes.
Jug with an incised representation of the fertility goddess.
Clay libation vessel with white decoration in the form of a goddess.

Terracotta figurine of a female figure with raised arms.

Stone offering-table, stone lamps and stone moulds for casting double axes.
Stone vases.
Perforated terracotta vessel for squeezing fruit.

Case 20
From the deposits at Gournes and Tylissos
Small libation jugs from the shrine deposit at Gournes Herakleiou.
Female figurine with a wide head-cover.
Bell-shaped figurines from Tylissos.
Heads of figurines with a characteristic high coiffure.
Jugs, skyphoi and cups from Tylissos.

Case 21
From the peak sanctuaries at Kophinas, Traostalos and Tylissos
Terracotta votive figurines of male and female worshippers.
Terracotta models of animals.
Terracotta models of ships and a fish.
Libation vases in the shape of bulls.
Stone altars or offering-tables.

Terracotta figurine of a male figure with a dagger at his waist.

Unnumbered case
From the peak sanctuary on Mount Juktas near Archanes (2000-700 BC)
Terracotta anthropomorphic and zoomorphic figurines.
Bronze anthropomorphic figurines.
Terracotta horns of consecration.
Bronze double axes.
Clay vases.
Clay mask.
Stone offering-tables, and a ladle. Some of the tables have inscriptions with a religious content.

Small unnumbered case
Finds from the peak sanctuary on Mount Juktas
Gold magical amulet with depictions of a scorpion, a snake and an insect.
Seals and gold and stone jewellery.

Case 22
From the old palace at Knossos
Cups, jugs and skyphoi in the polychrome Kamares style.

Terracotta figurine of a male figure with polychrome painted decoration.

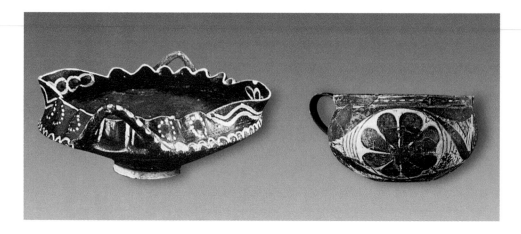

Kamares style egg-shell vases: left, a skyphos with two handles and a folded rim; right, a one-handled cup.

High-footed fruit-stand.
Next to the case stand some early sarcophagi with large numbers of handles, from the tomb at Voro.

Case 23
From the old palace at Knossos and the harbour-town at Poros

Jugs, skyphoi and cups in the Kamares style from the old palace at Knossos.
The egg-shell cups (cups with very thin walls) are masterpieces.
Bell-shaped figurine or model of a mask made of faience from Poros near Herakleion.
Small vase made of faience and gold.
Head of a terracotta figurine, possibly from a ritual vessel.

Case 24
From the peak sanctuaries at Petsophas Palaikastrou and Kalo Chorio Pediadas, and from the sanctuary in the palace at Knossos

Terracotta votive figurines of naked male figures.
Terracotta votive figurines of female figures.
Terracotta votive models of human limbs.
Terracotta models of altars with double horns.
Terracotta tricolumnar shrine with doves.
Terracotta model of a bier.
Terracotta bell-shaped figurines.

Kamares style tripod fruit-stand.

Case 25

Finds from the palaces at Malia and Knossos (1900-1700 BC)

Faience plaques depicting the facades of houses set in a landscape with animals and vegetation. They have been dubbed the "town mosaic" and possibly adorned a wooden box.

Clay rods, discs and tablets with ideograms.

Bronze dagger with a perforated gold handle.

Bronze figurines and gold bands from the peak sanctuary at Traostalos near Zakros.

Potsherds with relief marine motifs.

Clay sealings.

Kamares style large skyphos with three handles, a spout and a folded rim.

Case 26

From the palace and town of Malia and the town of Pseira

The clay pots are adorned with white paint on a lustrous red surface.

Vases with decoration of linked disks from Malia.

Vase with an undulating rim from Pseira.

Cups, a jug and a skyphos decorated with relief marine motifs.

Tripod fruit-stands.

Clay columns with models of birds sitting on them.

Jugs, skyphoi, amphoras and cups.
Skyphos with a relief monkey.
Bronze disc and bronze tripod basin.

Case 27
Large bridge-spouted vase in the early Kamares style.
Basin with polychrome decoration.
Amphoras with double axes.
Jug in the barbotine style with polychrome decoration.
Jugs and cups.

Case 27
Seals of the Old Palace period
Some of them have ideograms on the sealing surfaces.
Seals made of steatite in various shapes from the **cemetery of Prophitis Ilias, Knossos**. Jewellery from the same cemetery.
Seals from the **seal-engraving workshop at Malia**.
Seals from the **tombs of Apesokari** and **Kamilari**.

Case 29
Vases of the late Old Palace period from Knossos
Pithos decorated with a row of palm-trees.
Globular rhyton.
Foot of a fruit-stand decorated with double axes.
Large spouted amphoras.

Bronze dagger with a gold pierced cylindrical handle.

Faience plaques depicting trees and a wild goat, from the "Town Mosaic".

Faience plaques depicting house fronts, from the "Town Mosaic".

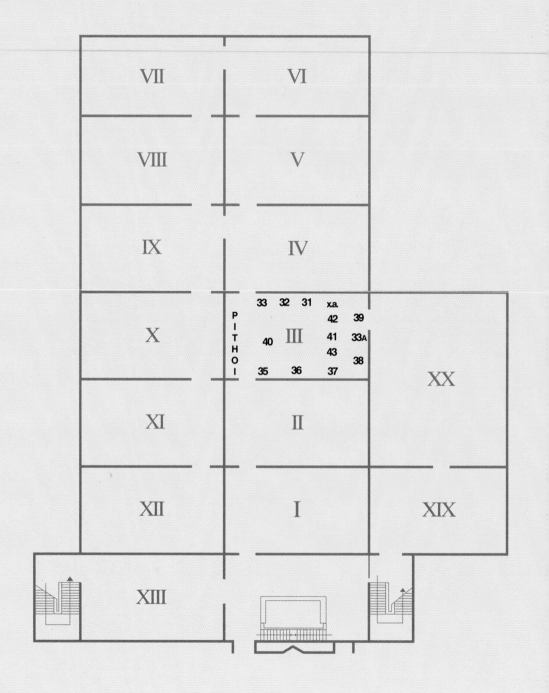

ROOM III

OLD PALACE PERIOD
THE PALACE AT PHAISTOS

The exhibits come from the first palace at Phaistos. The largest group consists of the beautiful polychrome Kamares ware vases. A few of the finds come from Anemospilia at Archanes and from the cave of Kamares. They include the fine fruit-stand and the krater with relief flowers, the unique clay Phaistos disc, a large number of functional and ritual clay and stone vases and vessels, and clay sealings from Phaistos. Also on display are the krater with the relief bull, the clay life-size feet of a statue, the iron ring and the bronze spear, from the temple of the human sacrifice at Anemospilia.

Case 35
Skyphoi and cups in the polychrome style from the **cult cave at Kamares** on the south slopes of Mount Ida, from which this style derives its name.
Bridge-spouted jug with a stylised octopus.
Oval-shaped perforated vessel for squeezing fruit.
Stone vase.

Kamares style one-handled cups decorated with white discs and wavy lines.

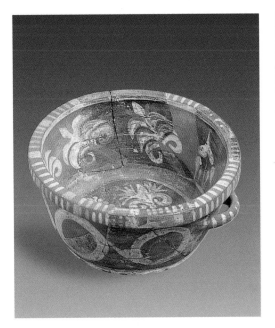

Kamares style two-handled bowl decorated with white lilies on the inside.

Unnumbered case

Cups, skyphoi, jugs, small jars, and a tray in the polychrome
Kamares style.
Clay vessel with a handle and an opening for carrying a lamp.
Stone vases.

Unnumbered case

Small pithos and bridge-spouted jugs in the polychrome Ka-
mares style.
Clay vase (basket) in the shape of a boat.
Egg-shell cups.
Jug with relief shell-fish.
Clay strainer.
Jugs with barbotine decoration.

Unnumbered case

Large skyphos with relief decoration of rosettes and a wild
goat.
Baskets, jugs, skyphoi with polychrome and barbotine decoration.

Kamares style one-handled
cup decorated with white spirals.

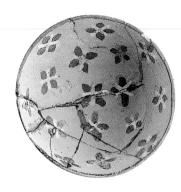

Kamares style bowl decorated with starfish on the inside.

Cup with folded rim.
Basin with decoration of white lilies on the interior.
Clay rhyton in the shape of a sow.
High-footed fruit-stand.
In the corner is a pithos in the Kamares style from Phaistos.
Pithoi with relief decoration from Anemospilia at Archanes.

Case 33A

Small pithoi, large skyphos, jug with polychrome and barbotine decoration.
Three-handled jugs with barbotine decoration.
Cups with polychrome decoration on the interior.

Kamares style rhyton with a handle, globular body and relief rim imitating a white lily.

Kamares style jug decorated
with spirals and other
curvilinear motifs.

Unnumbered case

Clay situla with relief and incised decoration rendering a bull
in a landscape, from the **temple at Anemospilia, Archanes**.

Case 98

Large Kamares style pithos with spiral decoration.
In the corner is a Kamares style pithos from **Phaistos.**

Unnumbered case

Skyphoi, jugs, baskets, globular rhyton, lantern, strainer in
the polychrome Kamares style.
Rhyton with a flower-shaped rim.
Stone kernoi, offering-tables and other vases and vessels.
Amphoriskos with human figures in a floral border.
Rhyton with white and barbotine decoration.

Kamares style bridge-
spouted deep skyphos.

Kamares style pithos decorated with fish, spirals and other curvilinear motifs.

Case 32

Bridge-spouted jugs, ordinary jugs, cups, amphora, strainer, feeding bottle with polychrome and barbotine decoration.
Egg-shell cups in the Kamares style.
Clay rhyta in the form of bulls.

Case 128

Cylindrical base of a lamp or fruit-stand with relief decoration of marine animals (dolphin, shells) and stylised rocks or waves.

Case 31

Cylindrical vase, pithoid vessel, a basket, jugs, cups.
Tall communion chalice.
Clay "wringer".
Stone cups, jug, basin, offering-table.

Kamares style fruit-stand decorated with spirals.

Kamares style three-handled jug with painted and barbotine decoration.

Case 36
Jugs, skyphoi and cups with folded walls and rims.
Clay basket.
Clay bull rhyton.
Vases influenced by metal models.
In the corners are Kamares style pithoi from the palace at Phaistos.

Case 43
Kamares style pithos with a scene of fish and nets.
Fruit-stand with rich painted and relief decoration.
Krater and jug with rich painted and relief decoration.

Case 41
The unique clay **Phaistos disc** with impressed ideograms or hieroglyphs. The inscription is arranged in a spiral running from the edge of the disc to the centre. Each sign indicates a syllable and the words are divided by vertical lines. The content remains an unsolved mystery.

Case 42
From the sanctuary in the palace at Phaistos
Figurines of human figures and monkeys and incised stone offering-tables.
Terracotta offering-tables.
Fruit-stand and bowl with a dance scene.
Conical rhyton with a relief wild goat.
Amphoriskos with a scene of a human figure.
Triton shell.

From Anemospilia, Archanes
Clay life-sized feet from a wooden statue.
Iron finger-ring.
Libation jug.
Agate seal with a scene of a boatman.
Bronze sword with a depiction of the face of a feline.

Cases 37, 40
Fragments from egg-shell and relief vases from the palaces of Knossos and Phaistos.
Parts of a terracotta figurine of a boar.
Clay sealings used to secure boxes, doors and vases, with decorative and pictorial motifs.
Discs incised with inscriptions in ideograms.
Clay tablet incised with the Linear A script.

Kamares style krater with white relief lilies.

The famous Phaistos disc (front).

The famous Phaistos disc (back).

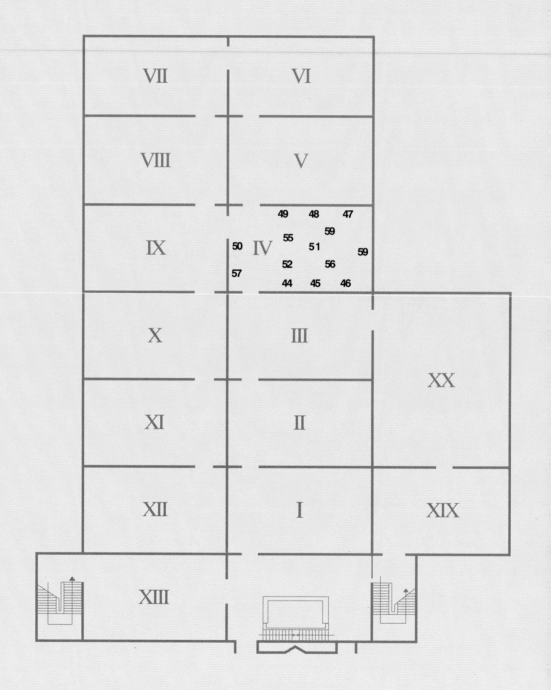

ROOM IV

NEW PALACE PERIOD (1700-1450 BC)
THE PALACES AT KNOSSOS, PHAISTOS AND MALIA

I n this room are displayed finds from the new palaces, the cities and the cemeteries of Knossos, Malia and Phaistos, from the Little Palace at Knossos, and from the tombs of Platanos Mesaras.

They include: clay vases in the floral and marine styles; clay and stone vases and vessels from the palace shrines; silver pins, cups and other vases with linear A inscriptions; and bronze tools and vases of everyday use.

There are some very fine examples of stonework and miniature art: the faience snake goddesses and the entire contents of the temple repositories of the palace at Knossos, the ivory acrobat, the rhytons in the shape of a bull's head and a lioness, and the royal gaming-board. The bronze swords with gold handles from Malia are unique.

Cup with floral style decoration.

Wide-mouthed jug with floral style decoration.

Cup with a Linear A inscription executed in a spiral in the inside.

Terracotta model of a honeycomb with a relief snake.

Case 44

Vases dating from the early New Palace period (1700-1600 BC) from **Knossos**, of the last phase of the Kamares style: deep skyphos, three-handled amphoras.

Jug with relief decoration of ears of barley.

Jug with floral style decoration and bands.

Tall amphora incised with a Linear A inscription.

Cups with Linear A inscriptions inside them, written with cuttle-fish ink.

Silver pins with incised Linear A inscriptions, from tombs at **Platanos Mesaras** and at **Ai-lia Knossou.**

Fragment of a head of a stone figurine.

Terracotta male figurine.

Tall vases with trickle decoration, in which the vase-painters allowed the paint to run down the surface of the vase.

Case 45

Jugs, cups and a bowl in the floral style.

Tall amphoras decorated with white lilies.

Clay lantern and an epinetron, a vessel for unwinding thread.

Vessel with receptacles, possibly to hold small libation cups.

Fragment of a cup decorated with an octopus.

Case 46

Clay tubular vessel with small cups attached to it, used for the cult of the sacred snake.
Terracotta model of a honeycomb with a snake.
Perforated clay vessels with relief snakes.
Cups with four handles, jugs and milk-jugs.
Cups, jugs and skyphoi in the floral style.
Vases decorated with double axes and sacral knots.
Stirrup-jar with scale-pattern decoration.

Case 58

Stone conical, oval and globular libation vessels (rhyta) made of alabaster, limestone and conglomerate from the **temple repositories of the palace at Knossos.** They have a hole at the bottom to allow the liquid to flow out slowly.
Stone model of a triton shell, rim of a stone rhyton, offering-table.

Case 47
Finds from the palace at Malia

Large bronze saw, bronze jug and basin with relief decoration of spirals, bronze two-handled basins.
Stone mace-head in the shape of an axe and a panther.
Part of a clay vessel with relief animals.

Bronze one-handled bowl with relief spiral decoration on the rim.

Piriform one-handled rhyton with marine style
decoration.

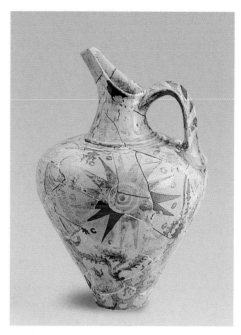

Jug with marine style decoration.

Cup with floral style decoration.
Jugs, stirrup-jars, and globular rhyton with spiral
decoration.
Clay double horns of consecration.

Case 48
Finds from the town of Malia
Stone lamps and offering-tables, stone cylindrical situla with
two-handles and a spout.
Jugs and alabastron in the marine style.
Stirrup-jar with spiral decoration.
Jugs and a footed cup from the final phase of the Kamares
style.

Case 49
Finds from the palace at Phaistos
Superb floral style oinochoe. Floral style footed cups and jug
with double axes and sacral knots.

Ephyrean kylix decorated
with a sacral knot.

Left:
faience figurine of the large
snake goddess.

Right:
faience figurine of the small
snake goddess.

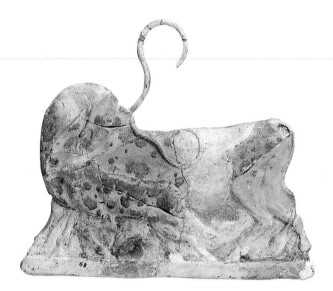

Relief faience plaque depicting a cow suckling her young.

Relief faience plaque in the form of a model of a garment.

Right, top:
gold sheathing from a sword-handle with an embossed depiction of an acrobat.

Right, bottom:
drawing of the depiction of the acrobat.

Jugs and cups with white decoration.
Rhyton in the shape of a bull's head.
Marine style rhyton with argonauts.
Figurine of a goddess or priestess in a posture of worship.
Stone offering-tables and small jugs with incised Linear A signs.
Sherds of pithoi and vases with incised Linear A signs.

Case 50
Finds from the temple repositories in the palace at Knossos
Faience figurines of the snake goddess (possibly mother and daughter). The figures are depicted with naked breasts and elaborately decorated clothing. The sacred snakes can be seen on their heads, arms and body, and in their hands.
Rosette of rock crystal, shells, models of flowers and marine animals of faience, which decorated the pedestal on which the figurines stood.
Small faience vases.
Stone offering-tables.

Case 57
Gaming board for a royal game resembling a form of chess, from the **palace at Knossos.** It is made of rock crystal, gold, and blue glass paste. The pieces are of ivory.

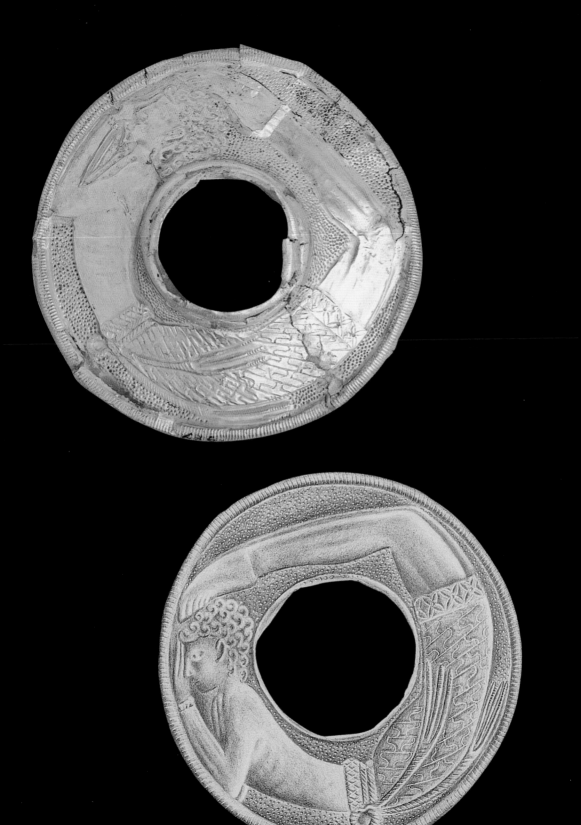

Part of a stone vase with a relief depiction of a shrine and adorants making offerings.

Part of the same vase with a depiction of an offering being made on the altar of a peak sanctuary.

Case 52
Finds from the palace at Malia
Royal sword from the palace at Malia, with a handle that was sheathed in gold and had a pommel of rock crystal.
Royal sword "of the acrobat", over which dangerous leaps were performed. The acrobat is portrayed on the gold sheathing of the handle.
Bronze mirror, vase and figurine of a sphinx.

Finds from the palace at Knossos
Parts of stone vases with relief ritual representations and athletic and martial scenes.
Crystal plaque with a depiction of a bull.
Plaque with a procession of priests wearing animal masks, from Phaistos.

Case 55
Finds from the temple repositories of the palace at Knossos
Stone cross, possibly an astral symbol.
Faience plaque depicting a cow and a wild goat suckling their young.
Faience models of garments.
Bronze weighing-scale pans and lead weights.
Part of an ivory sphinx with a crest on the head.
Fragments of relief stone vases.

Rock-crystal plaque with a painted depiction of a bull and bull-leaper.

Ivory figurine of a bull-leaper. Part of a large multifigural composition.

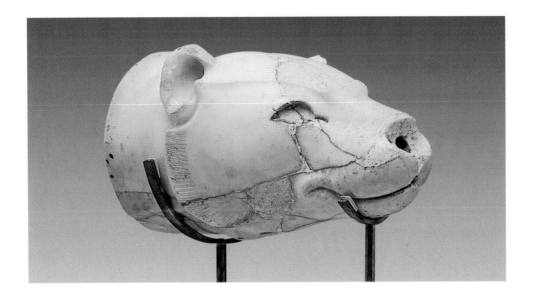

Stone rhyton in the shape of the head of a lioness, made of alabaster.

Case 51

Libation vase of steatite in the form of a bull's head, from a deposit in the **Little Palace at Knossos**. Restored at the left side. The eye is of crystal, the eyelid of jasper and the white muzzle of mother-of-pearl. One of the masterpieces of Minoan plastic art.

Case 56

The ivory figurine of the bull-leaper or acrobat. The hair was separately made of bronze. Anatomical details are rendered. The exaggeratedly long limbs render the tension of the movement. Parts of other, similar figurines are displayed along with it.

Case 60

Libation vessel in the form of the head of a lioness, of alabaster. The eyes and muzzle, which were separately made of a different material, have not survived. The lion is one of the animals that attended the deity, like the panther, etc.

In the north-east corner of the room is a large stone vase with a lid. In the north-west corner is a stone vase from the **palace at Knossos.**

Left:
stone rhyton in the shape of a bull's head, made of black steatite.

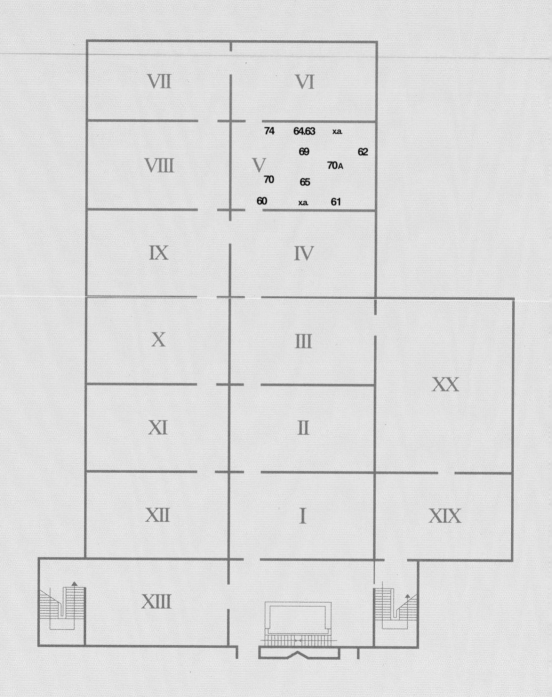

ROOM V

MATURE AND FINAL PHASES OF THE PALACE AT KNOSSOS
(1450-1300 BC)

R oom V contains finds from the new and final palace and city of Knossos, from the Unexplored Mansion, from Archanes, and from the tombs of the harbour town of Knossos at Poros-Katsambas.

They include: stone and clay palace-style vases and Ephyrean kylikes; jars and squat alabastra; stone architectural reliefs; and imported Egyptian vases and figurines. The clay model of a house is unique. The tablets incised with Linear A and Linear B inscriptions, the seals, the jewellery and other grave offerings give some idea of the artistic flowering in the palaces of the period.

Case 60

Jugs, cups, rhyta and stirrup-jars in the floral style from the houses on the Royal Road. They belong to the period just before the destruction of the palace in 1450 BC.
Double vase and stirrup-jar.

Unnumbered case

Basket, stirrup-jars, alabastron, jug in the floral style with spirals and shields.
Seals.
Wall-painting depicting wreaths, lilies and other flowers.

Case 61

Stone friezes with relief spirals, rosettes and semi-rosettes that adorned doorways in the palace.

Stone "ritual anchor" in the shape of a pyramid or wedge, made of porphyry and with relief decoration of an octopus. The object has also been interpreted as a weight standard for bronze talents.

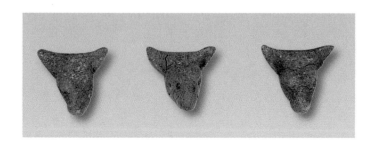

Faience necklace beads in the shape of a bull's head.

Stone lamp of porphyry, decorated with relief ivy leaves.

Pithos with palace style decoration of lilies.

Silver vessels from the **South House** at Knossos.
Bronze figurines from the **Little Palace** at Knossos.

Case 62
Porphyry lamps decorated with relief ivy leaves and papyrus
plants.
Stone fluted rhyton.
Anchor made of porphyry with a relief octopus.
Stone hair of a sphinx, the face of which is not preserved.
Imitation of rocks in porphyry, from a marine scene.
Imported Egyptian objects: lid of an alabaster pyxis with hi-
eroglyphs in a cartouche spelling the name of the Hyksos
Pharaoh Khyan, shallow bowls and a perforated stone jug.

Ritual jug with relief decoration
of a sacral knot.

Statuette of a seated figure of the Egyptian official Uzer.
Small stone poros head of eastern provenance.

Unnumbered case (at the right end of the north wall)
Finds from the Unexplored Mansion at Knossos (1500-1350 BC)
Jugs, skyphoi, Ephyrean kylikes, deep cups, footed cups, rhyton with stylised floral, scale-pattern and geometric decoration (palace style).
Jug with a scene of a male figure (see drawing).
Oval pyxis and large basket.
Terracotta figurine of a goddess.
Bronze figurine of a worshipper.

Cases 63, 64
Finds from the final phase of the palace at Knossos
Kraters, deep cups, kylikes in the palace style.
Terracotta double horns of consecration.
Stone tubular vessel and stone globular vase with a lid.
Stone tripod offering-table with legs in the shape of semi-rosettes.
Two-handled vase with spirals.

Case 74
Finds from the final phase of the palace at Knossos
Stone vases and vessels: lamp, offering-table, cup.
Clay alabastron decorated with an octopus.
Clay rhyton in the form of a bull's head.
Stone relief jug.
Clay jug with relief scale decoration and a sacral knot.
Stone squat alabaster.

Case 69
South side: clay tablets with incised Linear B inscriptions from the final phase of the palace at Knossos. They are page- or leaf-shaped and their contents relate to accounts (1450-1350 BC).
East side: clay tablets with incised Linear B inscriptions (1450-1350).

North side: clay tablets with incised Linear A inscriptions from Knossos, Phaistos, Tylissos, Zakros, Ayia Triada, Gournia and Lasithi (1700-1450 BC).

West side: fragments of vases with incised and painted Linear A inscriptions. Pieces of stone vases and vessels with incised

Clay tablets incised with Linear A (top) and Linear B (bottom) inscriptions.

Terracotta model of a single-storey brick house, showing many architectural details.

Linear A inscriptions. Stone ladle from Archanes with an incised Linear A inscription.

Case 65
New Palace seals from various sites.
Floral style and marine style sherds from **Knossos.**

Case 70
North side: jewellery, hammer-axe, boar's tusks, and a knife from the rock-cut **tomb at Poros.**

West side: members of ivory figurines – heads, arms, legs, torso – from **Archanes.**

Gold pendant in the form of a seated female figure.

South side: ivory objects – model of a house facade, dove, comb – from **Knossos.**

East side: fragment of a relief stone vase depicting a bull being caught in a net. Bronze figurine and fragments of ivory figurines from **Archanes.**

Case 70A
Clay model of a house from Archanes (1700-1500 BC)
On the west wall: four three-handled palace style jars from the palace at Knossos. In the centre is a pithos in the same style.

In the north-west corner: stone pithos with four handles and relief spirals.

In the south-west corner: three-handled amphora with relief spirals.

Case 67
Jewellery and other small objects from the cave-tombs at Poros near Herakleion.

South side: necklace with beads of coloured faience, gold pin with a sacral knot, broad gold cutout, gold earrings, faience bucrania, small gold figurine of a seated female figurine, and an ivory head of a male figurine.

West side: ivory mirror-handle, silver pins and earrings, necklace with beads of gold, semiprecious stones and faience, and gold finger-rings.

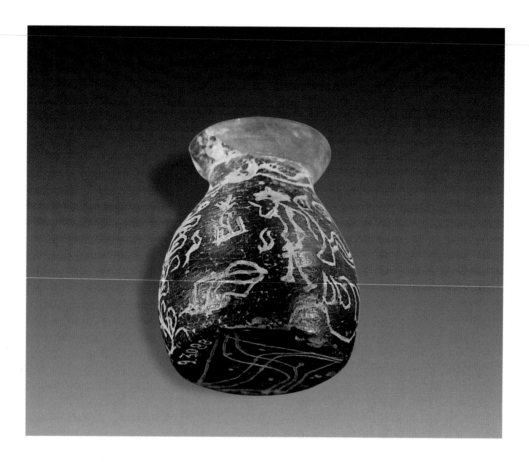

Clay alabastron-type vase with an incised depiction of a worshipper at an open-air altar.

North side: necklace with beads of precious stones, gold jewellery, hammer-axe, boar's tusks from a helmet, knife and a stone hammer-axe.

East side: finds from the jewellery workshop at **Poros,** the harbour town of Knossos.
Stone and clay moulds for casting jewellery, lead weights, unworked semiprecious stones, unfinished seals and beads.

Case 66
Grave offerings from the large cave-tombs and the harbour town of Knossos at Poros, dating from the mature Old Palace and the New Palace periods (1800-1500 BC).

Top shelf: cups and other vases with painted floral style decoration.

Second self down: libation jugs and cups with painted decoration in the mature Kamares style.

Second shelf up: libation jugs, double vase and other vases with painted floral style decoration.

Fragments of wall-paintings, terracotta bird figurines, small faience cups and a fragment of a relief vase.

Small alabastron-type vase with an incised scene of an adorant at on an open-air altar.

Bottom shelf: libation jugs and a double vase, stone tools, clay air-vent from a metal-working kiln, stone weight, and flint arrow-healds.

Twin piriform vase with strainer, with floral style decoration.

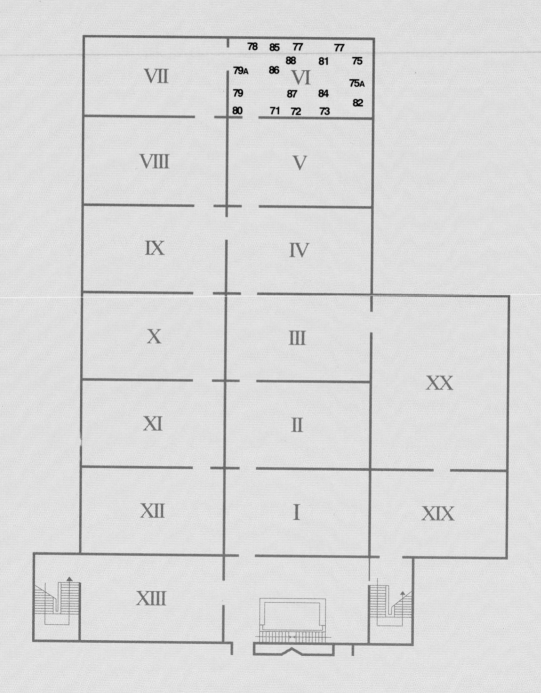

ROOM VI

THE CEMETERIES AT KNOSSOS, PHAISTOS AND ARCHANES

In this room are displayed the finds from the cemeteries of the palace cities of Knossos, Phaistos and Archanes, the harbour town of Knossos at Katsambas, and the tomb at Kamilari.

They include: clay models of a dance and of a funeral cult, from Kamilari; stone and clay vases from the royal tombs at Knossos; an alabaster Egyptian amphora; bronze grave offerings (weapons and a helmet) from the tombs at Knossos and Archanes; a boar's tusk helmet, the horse sacrifice from the royal tomb at Archanes; bronze weapons with gold handles; and gold and silver vases from the tombs of the warriors at Knossos.

The jewellery of gold, ivory, faience and precious stones is unique. We may note the gold signet-rings, the necklaces and the sealstones, and the relief ivory pyxis.

Terracotta model of four male figures performing a circular dance.

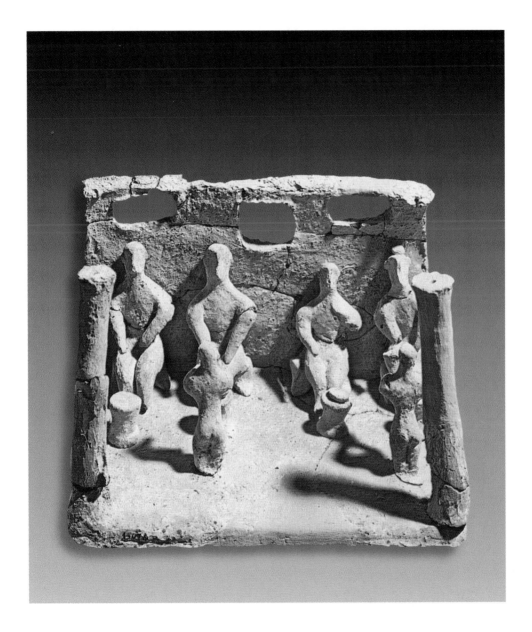

Terracotta model of a building with two columns, with seated figures inside it who are possibly persons deified after their death.

Alabastron-type vase with palace style decoration of a bird and a fish.

Alabastron-type vase with a depiction of an octopus.

Case 71
Finds from the tholos tomb at Kamilari, near Phaistos (1900-1300 BC)

Pottery of the Pre-palace period.

Clay model showing a circular dance performed by men in honour of the dead or the chthonic deity.

Clay model of a building with two columns. Inside it are two seated male figures, who are possibly heroised or deified dead persons. In front of them are altars on which worshippers are placing offerings.

Clay representation of a banquet in honour of the dead.

A figure is looking on through the opening. Clay doves and horns indicate that it is a religious scene.

Alabastron with a depiction of birds.

Jugs, amphoras, skyphos, cups, alabastra, three-handled vases in the floral style and alternating style.

Case 72

Finds from the royal tomb at Isopata near Knossos
Stone vases, alabastra, jug, lamp, cylindrical two-handled vase, lamps, shallow bowls and an aryballos.
Large vase made of green porphyry.

Finds from the south royal tomb-shrine at Knossos
Ephyrean kylikes.
Cylindrical alabaster vase with a relief figure-of-eight handle.
Alabaster footed drinking cup.
Clay jugs, amphora and two-handled flask.
Stone quintuple kernos.

Case 73

Finds from the cemeteries at Zapher Papoura and Mavro Spilio Knossou
Stone nest-shaped alabastron.
Stone rhyton.
Clay double basket, three-handled alabastron, bowl with handle, jugs, globular flask, miniature vases, stirrup-jar, three-handled jar.
Figurine of a kourotrophos and a female figurine.

Detail showing a bird and fish from the vase on this page.

Globular beak-spouted jug with a depiction of aquatic birds.

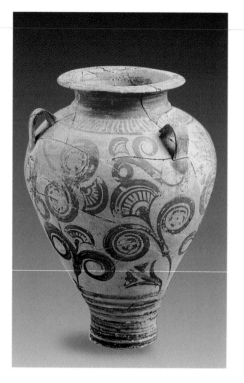

Jar with palace style decoration of papyrus flowers.

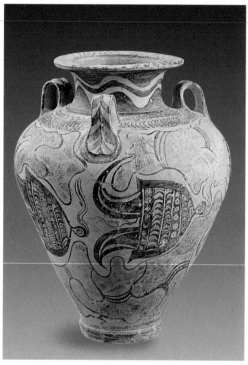

Jar with palace style decoration of helmets.

In the south-east corner is a three-handled, palace style amphora.

Case 82
Finds from tombs in the harbour-town of Knossos at Poros-Katsambas.
Palace style jar decorated with helmets.
Clay palace style globular jugs decorated with birds and flowers.
Clay braziers with charcoal.
Double vase with models of birds and floral decoration.
Stone alabaster vase, and a vase with a flat rim.
Oval alabaster amphora with a cartouche of the Pharaoh Tuthmoses III.

Case 75A
Tholos tomb A at Phourni, Archanes
Dismembered skeleton of a sacrificed horse.

Terracotta figurine of a kourotrophos goddess raising the "divine infant" in her arms.

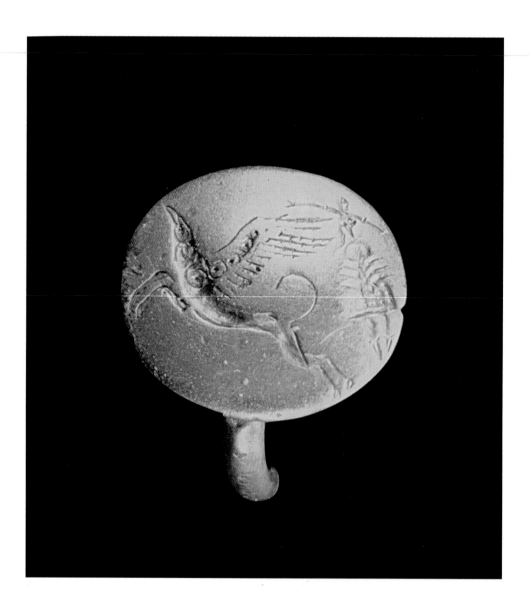

Gold finger-ring with a depiction of a goddess and a winged griffin.

Case 75
Finds from Tholos tomb A at Phourni, Archanes (top shelf)
Bronze vessels. Tripod cauldron, large jug, tripod bowl, jugs, lamps, sword, two-handled deep cups.
Clay cup, kylix and stone vases.

Finds from the Tomb of the Tripod Hearth at Zapher Papoura near Knossos
Bronze vessels. Large tripod cauldron, bowls with vertical handles, lamp, spoons, jugs, cup, tripod bowl.
Stone alabaster rhyton.

Case 76
Finds from tombs in the area of Knossos
Palace style jars, ritual vases with figure-of-eight handles, jugs, three-handled squat alabastra.
Stone vases, alabastron, stone skyphos, sword pommel (or club-head).
Bronze spearhead and double axes.

Case 77
Finds from the tombs at the Venizeleion Sanatorium and Ayios Ioannis near Knossos
Jugs, alabastra, palace style skyphos, Ephyrean kylikes.
Alabaster jug, stone relief vase in the shape of a flower, with a lid.
Stone model of a cuirass.
Silver footed cup and silver pin.
Bronze swords, spearheads, tongue-shaped daggers. arrowheads.
Gold cup with relief spiral decoration.

Case 81
Finds from tombs in the area of Knossos
South side: finds from tombs at Sellopoulo
Ivory objects: pyxis lid with relief figure-of-eight shields and papyrus flowers, model of a ship, mirror handle with a relief sphinx.
Scarab.
Gold finger-rings with a bezel and ring.
Necklace with gold beads in the shape of nautilus argonauts, hearts and papyrus flowers.

North side: finds from tombs at Zapher Papoura
Bronze mirrors, razors, tweezers, knife, pin.

Boar's tusk helmet,   Bronze helmet with cheekpieces.

Necklaces with beads of faience and semiprecious stones.
Ivory comb.
Sword pommel of rock crystal.

West side
Gold diadems.
Comb, game pieces, knuckle-bones, rosette, spindlewhorl and
figure-of-eight shield made of ivory.
Necklace with faience beads in the shape of a rosette.
Stone spindle-shaped missiles.

East side
Bronze knife, spearhead and sword.

Case 84
**Finds from tombs at the Venizeleion Sanatorium and Ayios
Ioannis near Knossos.**

North side
Long bronze swords, two with gold-sheathed handles decorated with scenes of lions chasing wild goats.

Ivory pyxis with a relief depiction of a bull-hunt.

Gold arrowhead.
Bronze spear- and arrowheads.

East side
Bronze spearheads.

South side:
Sword with a gold-sheathed handle decorated with a network
of spirals.
Bronze sword with an ivory handle.
Bronze swords, daggers and knives.
Bronze arrowheads.

West side:
Bronze spears and spearheads.

Case 85
Bronze helmet from a **tomb at the Venizeleion Sanatorium
near Knossos**

Case 78
Boar's tusk helmet from a **tomb at Zapher Papoura near
Knossos**

Case 86
Finds from tombs at Kalyvia and Kamilari near Phaistos
Gold necklaces and earrings.
Necklaces with beads of faience, glass paste and coloured stones.

Case 79A
Cylindrical ivory pyxis with a relief scene depicting the cap-
ture of a bull, from a tomb in the harbour-town of Knossos
(Katsambas).

Case 79
Small jar, stirrup-jars, alabastra and a basket.
Stone lamp, alabastron, alabaster triton-shell and globular
vase.
Faience amphora.

Case 80
Finds from the cemetery at the Harbour of Knossos
Libation jug with relief (figure-of-eight shield and sacral knot)
and painted decoration (argonauts and papyrus flowers).

Gold finger-ring with a depiction of a sacred dance.

Case 87
Finds from the cemeteries at Knossos, Phaistos and elsewhere
Necklaces with gold beads of various shapes.
Gold signet-ring with a scene of the 'reception' of the goddess.
Gold 'mask' from Mouliana.
Earrings in the shape of a bull's head from Olous.
Gold finger-ring from Praisos.

Case 88
Finds from the cemetery at Phourni, Archanes
Necklaces with gold beads of various shapes.
Necklaces with beads of sardius and glass paste in various shapes.
Gold signet-ring with a scene of mourning for the youthful god of vegetation, or the sacred tree cult.
Gold finger-rings with scenes of shields and sacral knots.
Bronze mirror with ivory handle.
Parts of the ivory decoration of a wooden box: shields, stylised trees, heads of warriors, depictions of bulls and lions.

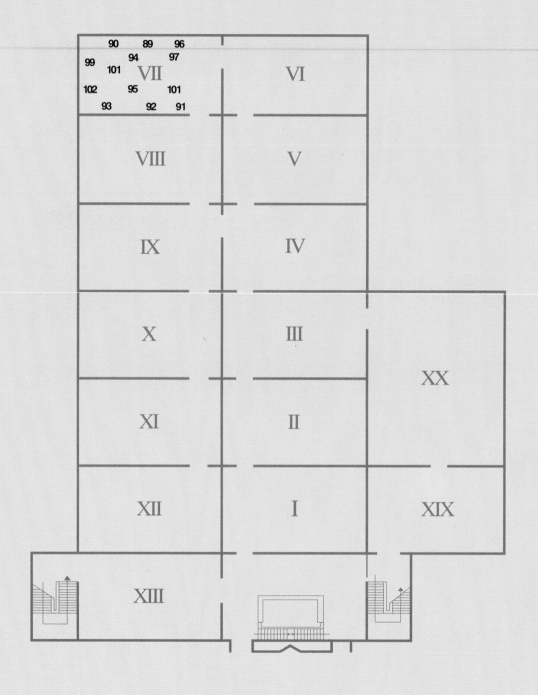

ROOM VII

THE PALACE AT AYIA TRIADA
THE MEGARA AT VATHYPETRO, NIROU CHANI, TYLISSOS AND AMNISOS
THE CAVES AT ARKALOCHORI, PSYCHRO AND PATSOS
THE CEMETERIES AT MALIA, MOCHLOS, GOURNIA AND EPISKOPI

The display in this room consists of finds from the palace at Ayia Triada near Phaistos, from the megara at Nirou, Vathypetro, Tylissos and Amnisos, from the Diktaean cave, and the cult caves at Skoteinos and Patsos, and the cave at Arkalochori. Also from the cemeteries of Phaistos, Malia, Mochlos and Episkopi Pediadias.

They include: huge bronze cult axes and stone horns of consecration; relief steatite vases; clay and stone vases and vessels; bronze figurines; cult objects; bronze swords; and bronze and clay tools and implements of everyday use.

The gold jewellery (note the ornament with the bees), the votive gold axes and the gold signet-rings are outstanding.

Left:
part of the rhyton on the opposite page, with a relief depiction of a boxing match.

Right:
detail of the same rhyton with a depiction of a helmeted boxer.

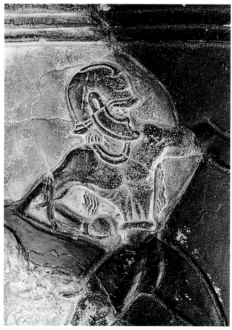

Conical rhyton of black
steatite with four relief
scenes, of wrestling, boxing
and bull-leaping.

The same figurine from the side. The adorant's body is arched like a bow.

Left:
bronze figurine of a male figure in an attitude of reverence, with his clenched fist held to his forehead.

Bronze figurine of a male figure from the Diktaean Cave.

East corner
Large bronze cult axes from the **megaron at Nirou** (1700-1500 BC).
Double horns of consecration from the **megaron at Nirou**.

Case 96
Steatite rhyton with relief scenes of bull-leaping and boxing, from the **palace at Ayia Triada**.

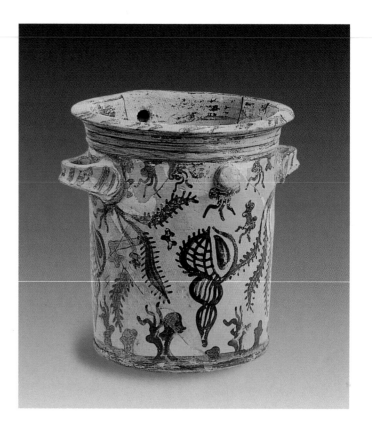

Cylindrical vase with marine style decoration.

Case 89
Middle shelf: finds from the Minoan megara at Tylissos
Bronze figurines of worshippers.
Obsidian rhyton.
Jugs, cups and a jar.

Top and bottom shelves: finds from the Minoan megaron at Nirou
Cylindrical marine style vase.
Amphoras and skyphos in the floral style.
Stone lamps.

Case 90
Finds from the megara at Sklavokambos, Tylissos, Vathypetro and Amnisos
Bridge-spouted vase, stone rhyton and perforated vessel.

Stone lamps, large cup, cylindrical vase, fruit-stand.
Stone vases, floral style vases.
Head of a poros figurine.

Case 99
Bronze talent in the shape of a double axe, from the **palace at Ayia Triada.**

Case 102
Finds from the Minoan palace at Ayia Triada
Stone communion chalice, rhyton, lamp, model of a reclining sphinx, alabastron, model of a seated monkey.
Large terracotta figurine of a female figure with multiple breast-like protrusions on her body.
Alabaster model of a boat.
Terracotta female figurines.
Bronze figurines of women, men and animals.

Case 93
Finds from the Minoan palace at Ayia Triada
Alabastra, jugs, cups, a skyphos, amphora, jar, and a lamp.
Figurines of a man, woman, and a bird on double horns.
Trays with carbonised seeds of wheat, pulses and figs.

Case 92
Finds from the cult caves at Psychro (Diktaean Cave), Skoteinos and Patsos
Jug, cups, kylix, figurine and head of a figurine.
Bronze double axes and knives.
Bronze figurines of men, women and animals.
Bronze Egyptian figurine.
Offering-table, sherds from relief pithoi, pieces of a bull rhyton.
Double stone horns of consecration.

Case 91
Finds from the cave at Arkalochori
Bronze double axes, one of them with a pseudo-hieroglyphic inscription.

Case 101
West side: finds from the cave at Arkalochori
Bronze and silver axes, sheets, and pins.

Jug decorated with double axes and sacral knots.

South side: finds from tombs near Phaistos, Episkopi, and Gournia (1600-1400 BC)

Gold jewellery, lion, fish, duck and eye.
Gold signet-ring with a cult scene.
Gold earrings, rosettes, necklaces, pins.
Tiny figurine of a seated female.

East side: finds from tombs at Chrysolakkos, Malia and Mochlos

Gold pendant with bees.
Gold pin with a head in the shape of a flower.
Gold signet-ring bearing a scene of a sacred ship with the goddess and the tree.
Gold earrings, amulets, pin-head, beads.

North side

Tiny gold amulet with a spiral, spider, snake, scorpion, and a human hand.
Gold jewellery in the form of heads of oxen and lions.
Gold finger-rings, amulets and necklaces.

Case 94

Relief steatite rhyton with a scene of a procession of harvesters, from the **palace at Ayia Triada.**

Case 95

Relief steatite cup with a scene of an official and a procession of men.

Case 97
North side: Tylissos, Nirou, and Malia

Bronze, ivory and steatite figurines.

East, south and west sides: the cave at Arkalochori

Long bronze swords, daggers, double axes, subdivisions of bronze talents.

Case 100

Bronze double axes/tools.
Clay potter's wheels.
Parts of an ivory pyxis with incised decoration.
Bronze tools: wheels, chisels, axes.
Bronze saws, daggers, mattock, weighing scale.
Bronze saw.

Gold votive double axes with incised linear decoration.

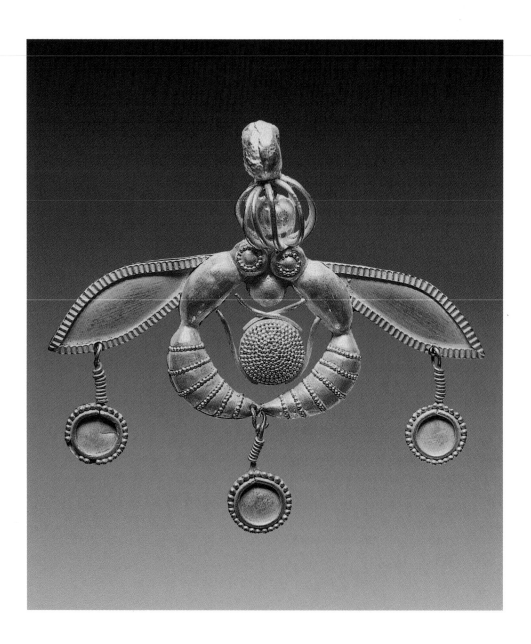

Gold ornament in the form of two bees holding a honeycomb between their legs.

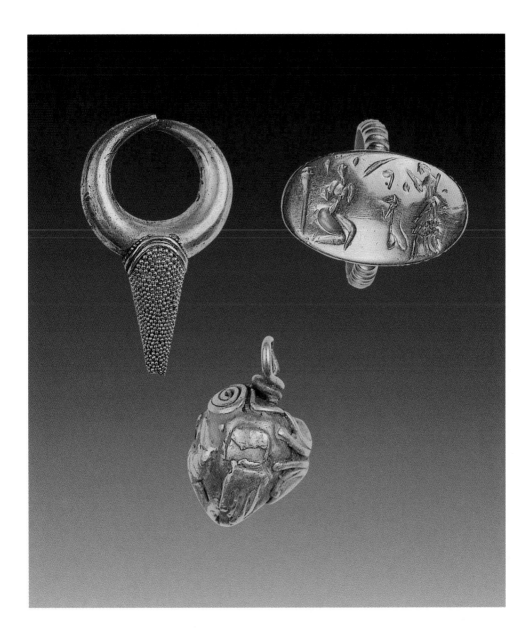

Gold earring, gold signet-ring and a tiny amulet with a spiral, scorpion, spider, snake and arm.

The famous steatite relief
vase with a depiction of
harvesters.

Detail of the scene of the harvesters on the vase on the opposite page.

Black steatite vase known as the "Cup of the Report" or "Cup of the Chieftain".

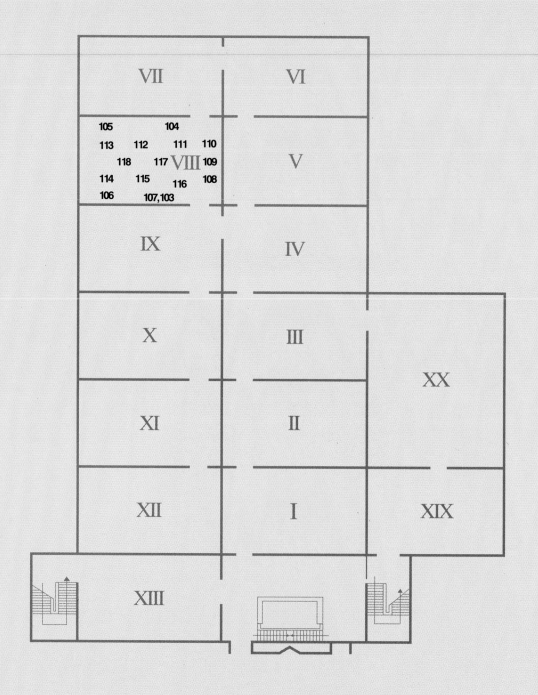

ROOM VIII

THE PALACE AT ZAKROS

This room contains the important finds from the fourth of the Minoan palaces, excavated at Zakros in the 1960s. Fate has preserved all its fittings and equipment, since it was never plundered.

They include: the unique rock-crystal rhyton with gold sheathing decorated with a relief representation; clay and stone rhyta; a libation rhyton in the shape of a bull's head; clay rhyta in the shape of a bull and a bull's head; bronze talents; ivory; and a large number of bronze tools, vessels and vases. Also pithoi with incised Linear A inscriptions and a relief frieze with spirals, which decorated the walls of the palace.

Alabaster rhyton in the form of a triton shell.

Case 111
Rhyton of chlorite with the remains of the gold sheathing. The differences in colour are due to the fire that destroyed the palace. It has a relief depiction of a peak sanctuary in a rocky landscape with mountain vegetation, birds and wild goats.

Case 104
Ritual libation vessel with large figure-of-eight handles and holes in the top. Circular tubular rhyton.

Case 112
Bronze axe with double blades and decoration of stylised lilies and holes.
Bronze swords, axes, pairs of tongs, hammer.

Case 105
Clay vases. Clay funnel with floral style decoration.
Stone vases, lamps, poros offering-table, steatite model of a triton shell.
Bronze vases and vessels.
Bronze censer (or brazier) decorated with ivy leaves.

Case 113
Bronze talents in the shape of double axes. The metal was imported in this form from Cyprus.
Elephant tusks, probably from Syria. Raw material for the

Piriform rhyton of chlorite with a relief depiction of a peak sanctuary.

Detail of the depiction on the rhyton, showing seated wild goats.

Communion chalice, made of
obsidian imported from the
island of Yiali near Nisyros.

manufacture of small works of art.

Stirrup-jars and rhytons in the marine style, with octopuses,
triton shells, rocks and seaweed.

Floral style cups.

Marine style oinochoe with a large number of small argonauts.

Fragment of a rhyton in the form of a bull's head with gilded
nostrils.

Case 118

Hoard of stone ritual vases and vessels from the shrine repository.

Limestone jug with a double mouth and S-shaped handles.

Faience bull's heads (rhyta).

Communion cups for offerings to the deity.

Egyptian vases.

Ritual hammers.

Case 117

Small ivory objects that decorated wooden boxes: quadruple
axes, small butterfly, sea-shells.

Small clay head of a wildcat.

Flask decorated with a white
rosette in the late Kamares
style.

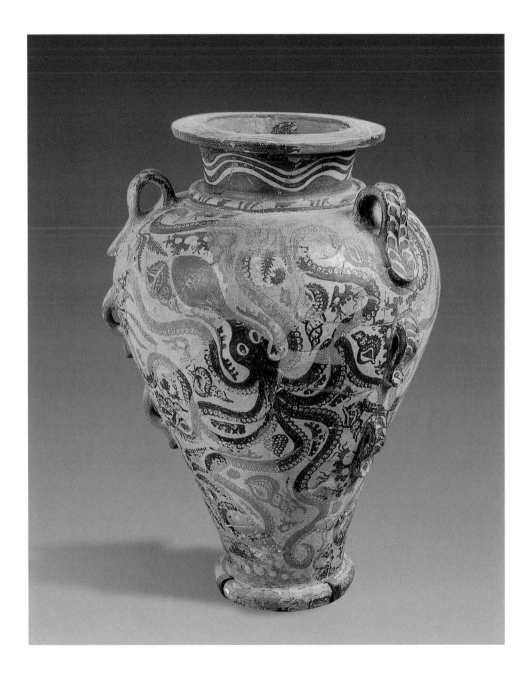

Jar with palace style decoration of an octopus.

Silver vessel, gold ring, small silver spoon.
Faience vase in the shape of a sea-shell.
Clay head of a feline.
Fragment of a stone rhyton.

Case 114
Conical stone rhyta from the shrine repository.
Bridge-spouted jugs and cups with lugs and handles on the interior.

Case 106
Conical and oval clay rhyta, the former with marine style and the latter with floral style decoration.
Stone lamp of chlorite.
Clay amphora.
Clay fruit-stand.

Stone amphora with a double mouth and S-shaped handles, made of pieces of limestone.

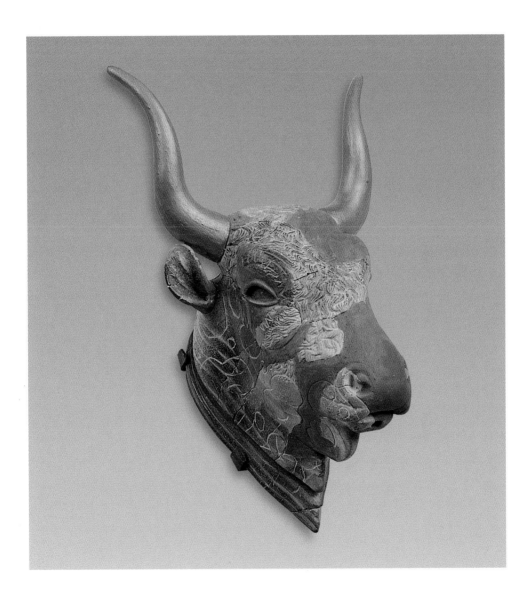

Case 115

Large bronze saw with wooden handles at both ends.

Two smaller bronze saws found bent double.

Bronze handles and legs of large cauldrons, hammers, double axes and spearheads.

Rim of a large bronze disc decorated with double axes.

Square sheets of bronze worked in relief.

Stone rhyton in the shape of a bull's head, of chlorite.

Cases 107, 103

Jugs and footed cups in the floral style, or with spiral decoration and with white paint.

Tall oinochoe with relief decoration, used for libations.

Next to case 107

Three-handled marine style amphora with a scene of an octopus amongst sea-shells, seaweed and rocks.

Case 116

Libation vessel (rhyton) in the form of a bull's head, smaller than the similar vase from Knossos. The pouring hole is in the muzzle. The horns have been restored.

Case 110

Finds from the old excavations at Zakros and Palaikastro

Marine style rhyton with star-fish, sea-shells, rocks and seaweed.

Clay head of a wild goat, part of a terracotta figurine.

Amphoras, deep cups, rhyta, a flask with a white star-fish, and a strainer of the 17th c. BC, the final phase of the polychrome Kamares style.

Floral style cups.

Clay rhyton with barbotine decoration.

Stone vases.

Outside this case are displayed pithoi with incised Linear A inscriptions.

Case 109

Superb rhyton of rock crystal with a gilded ring at the neck, and handle consisting of spherical crystal beads threaded on bronze wire.

Case 108

Clay rhyta, cups and amphoras decorated with double axes and spirals.

Oval rhyton with a relief ring around the mouth and relief sacral knots.

Pair of small stone horns.

Small stone figurine.

Small stone column capital with an integral abacus.

Stone cup of alabaster.

Opposite page:
superb rhyton, made of rock crystal with bronze on the handle and gold at the neck.

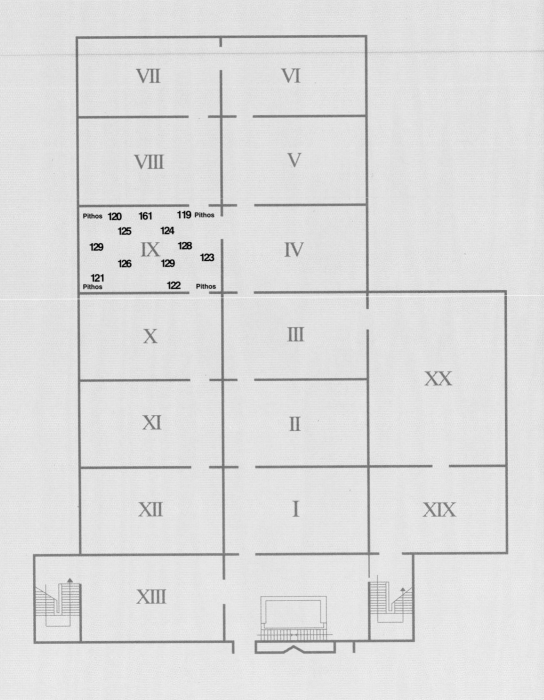

VII

VI

VIII

V

Pithos 120   161   119 Pithos

125   124

129   IX   128

126   129   123

121
Pithos   122   Pithos

IV

X

III

XX

XI

II

XII

I

XIX

XIII

ROOM IX

THE NEW PALACE PERIOD IN EAST CRETE
PALAIKASTRO, PSEIRA, GOURNIA, PISKOKEPHALO, MOCHLOS
AND MYRTOS

T his room contains finds from the important Mi-
noan centres in east Crete: the town of Palaikastro,
Pseira, Gournes and Mochlos on the bay of Mirambello,
Myrtos, and the sanctuary at Piskokephalo Siteias.

They include: clay marine style rhyta; stone vases, vessels and tools; rhyta in the shape of a bull and a bull's
head; and bronze figurines, tools and implements.

Visitors may note especially the ivory figurines and jewellery in a variety of materials; the clay sealings; the sealstones of semiprecious stone; the terracotta figurines of
men and women with their elegant coiffures; and the
clay models of the sacred insect, the *oryctes nasicornis*
beetle.

Two-handled vase with a thin
wall and folded rim, with similar small cups inside it.

Detail of the vase on this page, showing a bucranium.

Jar decorated with bucrania and double axes.

Case 119
Finds from Palaikastro
Stone lamps and offering-table of porphyry and steatite.
Stone vases and stone pestle.
Clay rhyton in the form of a bull's head.
Clay grill, clay funnel and twin vases.
Terracotta male figurine.
Bronze human and animal figurines.

Case 161
Finds from Myrtos (Pyrgos)
Jugs, cups and skyphoi.
Clay tubular cult vessels with relief decoration.
Two-handled cup with black surface and folded rim, in which many similar, tiny vases are incorporated.

Faience model of a triton-shell.
Stamped handles of vases.
Stone vases and stone hammer.
Bronze dagger.
Steatite seals, clay sealings and fragment of a Linear A tablet.

Case 120
Finds from Palaikastro
Stone kernos for making multiple offerings, and stone vases.
Vase in the shape of a flask with a depiction of an octopus.
Oval rhyta, jugs, cups, alabastron.
Terracotta heads of felines.
Fragment of a vase of rock crystal.

Flask with marine style
decoration of an octopus.

Case 125
Finds from Palaikastro

Clay marine style libation vessels (rhyta)
Stone offering-tables and stone model of a triton-shell.
Globular stirrup-jar with a depiction of an octopus.
Conical rhyton with painted and relief decoration and a head of a wild goat in place of the handle.
Oval and globular stone tools. One has a fish engraved on it.
Cylindrical vases with holes in the walls.
Stirrup-jars, deep cups, jugs.
Clay model of the *oryctes nasicornis* beetle.

Case 129
From the New Palace town at Mochlos

Small pithoi with lids and spouts.
Stone lamps.
Bronze bowls with handles. One has spiral decoration around the edge.
Clay rhyta in the form of a bull and a bull's head.
Clay alabastron, cups and jugs.

Case 126
Finds from Gournia

Large stone lamps. Conical stone rhyton worked in relief.

Rhyton with marine style decoration of starfish, nautilus argonauts, etc.

Vase in the shape of a basket with two large handles, decorated with four zones of double axes.

Conical bases for double axes.

Clay conical, globular and oval rhyta.

Stone offering-tables and other stone vessels and tools.

Bronze tripod cauldron.

Case 121

Finds from Gournia

Double vases and stirrup-jars, cylindrical pithoid vases, jugs, alabastron, tripod pyxis.

Clay rhyton in the form of a bull's head.

Bronze figurine of a worshipper in an attitude of worship.

Silver cup with folded rim and two handles.

Case 122

Finds from Pseira

Globular stirrup-jar with a depiction of an octopus.

Clay models of bulls.

Stone communion cup, stone lamps and stone hammer.

Rhyton made of conglomerate.

Clay marine style rhyton. Globular jugs.

Clay basket decorated with double axes.

Case 127

Bronze tools: double and single axes, swords, fish-hooks, razors, scrapers, chisels, tweezers, knives and pickaxes from Zakros, Palaikastro, Siteia, Pseira, Mochlos, Gournia and Ayia Triada.

Clay sealings with portraits of a mature ruler and a young prince, and inscriptions in an ideogrammatic script.

Case 124

Clay sealings from many sites in Crete: Ayia Triada, Zakros, Palaikastro, Gournia, Sklavokambos and Tylissos (1600-1400 BC)

Sealings were used to seal objects. The seal was impressed on small pieces of wet clay. Motifs on seals include birds, animals, cult scenes, sanctuaries, deities, chariots and imaginary daemons (sealings from Zakros).

Ivory plaques with a variety of scenes from Palaikastro.

Clay head of a feline.

Clay palmette mould.

Ivory figurines of children from Palaikastro.

Jewellery made of coloured stones.

Bronze pin.

Lenses of rock crystal.

Stone figurine of a monkey, of steatite.

Sealstone of azurite set in gold,
depicting a lion and a male figure.

Engraved prismatic amulet of
black steatite.

Lentoid sealstone of sardonyx,
depicting a goddess between
two griffins.

Elliptical sealstone of
chalcedony with a depiction of
a wild goat on a rock.

Prismatic sealstone of
steatite with a depiction of
reptiles.

Sealings from Knossos with hieroglyphic inscriptions and depictions of people.

Left:
lentoid sealstone of chalcedony with a depiction of a lion tearing apart a bull.

Right:
elliptical sealstone of chalcedony with a depiction of a wild goat on a rock.

Case 128
Seals of the New Palace period (1700-1400 BC). The materials are hard, semiprecious stones: agate, haematite, lapis lazuli, chalcedony, meteorite, sardonyx, jasper and amethyst.
The predominant shapes are lentoid, amygdaloid and cylindrical.
On the sealing surfaces are depicted animals, wild goats, lions tearing apart bulls, griffins, octopuses, cuttle-fish, deities, imaginary beings, and flowers.

Case 123
From the peak sanctuary at Piskokephalo near Siteia
Figurines of male and female figures in an attitude of worship, with the arms held close to the body or folded across the breast.
There is great variety in the coiffures of the figurines.
Models of shrines surmounted by horns of consecration.
Model of the sacred insect, the *oryctes nasicornis* beetle, with a horn.

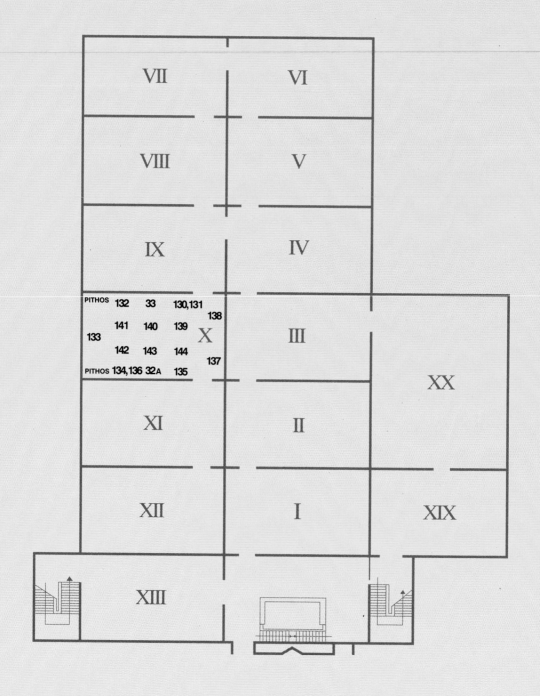

PITHOS 132   33   130,131
                            138
        141   140   139
133   X   III
        142   143   144
                            137
PITHOS 134,136 32A   135

ROOM X

POST-PALACE PERIOD (1400-1100 BC)

In this room are exhibited objects from the final period of the Minoan civilisation, from the towns of Knossos, Phaistos, Archanes and Palaikastro, from the Minoan sanctuaries at Katsambas, Gazi near Herakleion, and Metropoli Gortynas, and from the cemeteries at Phinikia near Herakleion, Karteros, Gournes, Episkopi and Stamnies, and Mouliana Siteias.

They include: clay vases in the style of the period, with stylised decoration; large terracotta figurines with raised arms; other terracotta figurines; clay cult vessels and vases; and a group of terracotta figurines depicting women dancing to the accompaniment of the lyre.

Case 130
From the deposit at Katsambas and the tombs at Phinikia near Herakleion
Clay rhyton, footed kylikes and cups from the shrine deposit at Poros-Katsambas.
Vases from the chamber tomb at Phinikia.

Case 131
Finds from the final phase of the palace at Knossos (reoccupation period, 14th c. BC)
Stirrup-jar decorated with a stylised octopus.
Flask decorated with concentric circles.
Bronze vessel.

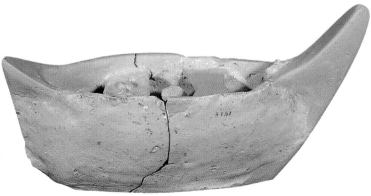

Terracotta model of a boat.

Figurines of dancers performing a circular dance, with the musician playing the lyre in the middle.

Case 132
Finds from Palaikastro
Group of terracotta figurines depicting female figures, holding each other by the shoulder and dancing. In the middle is a musician playing a lyre.
Clay incense-burner, with the lid decorated with birds.
Small stirrup-jars and jugs.
Pyxis decorated with birds.

Case 133
Figurines of female figures from the sanctuary at Gazi near Herakleion
The bodies are stylised. The dress is treated as a cylinder. The arms are raised in a gesture of greeting or blessing.
They have various symbols on the heads: birds, horns and flowers of the *papaver soporificus* poppy.

Figurine of a goddess with raised arms, with brown painted decoration.
On her head are models of horns of consecration and figurines of birds.

The "poppy goddess". Large figurine of a goddess with raised arms.
On her head are models of the *papaver soporificus* poppy.

Case 134

Finds from tombs at Episkopi and Stamnies Pediadas
Clay jugs, stirrup-jars, kylikes.
Stone kernos.
Bronze vases.

Case 135

Finds from the Minoan sanctuary at Mitropoli Gortynas
Terracotta figurines of deities with raised arms and conical
head-coverings, on which can be seen the heads of snakes.
Terracotta female figurine with snakes in her hands and a
small dove on her head.
Clay tubular libation vessels decorated with relief heads of a
bull and a wild goat.
Stone altar in the shape of a column.
Small plaque with a relief sphinx, and an altar with the sacred
tree.

Case 136

**Finds from tombs at Mouliana Siteias and Episkopi Iera-
petras**
Large flask, stirrup-jars, lid of an incense-burner, and jugs
decorated with bands and stylised octopuses.

Case 137

**Finds from tombs at Karteros and Gournes Pediadas and
Pachyammos Ierapetras**
Clay incense-burner with a perforated lid.
Clay composite vessel and double horns.
Clay jewellery box (pyxis) decorated with birds.
The contents of the pyxis: necklaces with beads made of glass
paste, and gold finger-rings.

Case 138

Finds from the towns of Knossos, Phaistos and Archanes
Double clay vases, found together with Linear B tablets at the
north entrance to the palace at Knossos.
Terracotta figurines from Phaistos. Clay model of a horse car-
rying amphoras.
Terracotta figurine of a goddess riding on a horse, from
Archanes.
Terracotta figurine of a horse with a yoke on its back.
Terracotta child coffins.

Terracotta figurine of a
"goddess" seated on a horse.

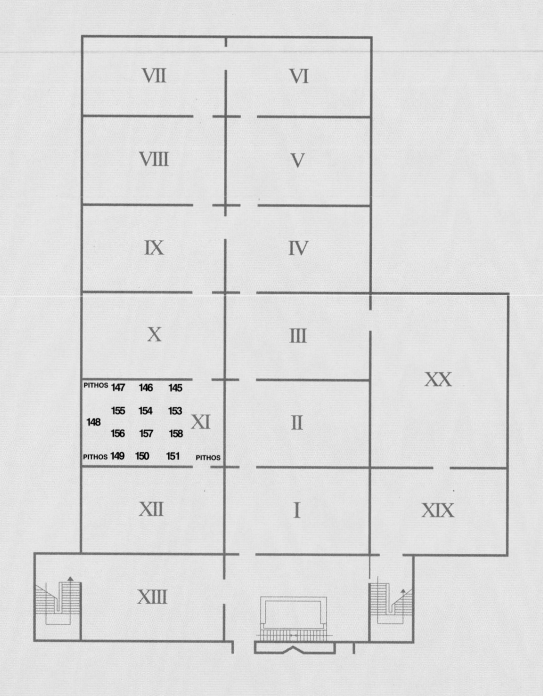

ROOM XI

SUB-MINOAN, PROTOGEOMETRIC AND
EARLY GEOMETRIC PERIODS (1100 - 800 BC)

Finds from the transitional phase between the Minoan and Geometric periods, and also from the Protogeometric and Geometric periods, mainly from the settlements at Karphi Lasithiou, Vrokastro and Kavousi in the bay of Mirambello, the cult cave of Eileithyia at Inatos (Tsoutsouros), and the cemeteries of Phaistos and Kourtes Mesaras, Tekes and Fortetsa near Knossos, and Prinias.

They include: cinerary urns (cremation was widespread at this period) and other clay vases in the Protogeometric and Geometric styles with linear motifs; large terracotta figurines of the Minoan goddess with raised arms; bronze and terracotta figurines of men and women; models of various animals and objects; and figurines and a faience scarab imported from Egypt.

Clay kernos consisting of a ring with amphoriskoi and figurines attached to it.

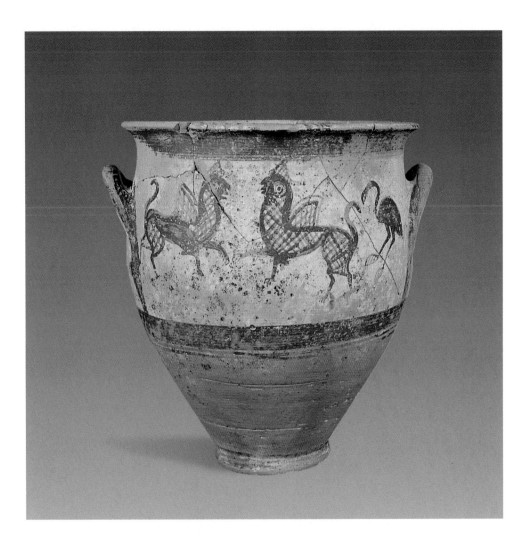

Krater decorated with wild goats and aquatic birds.

Case 145

Finds from the cemeteries at Phaistos and Kourtes Zarou

Ring-shaped kernos with small amphoras and human figures.

Case 146

Finds from the settlement and cemetery at Vrokastro

Cinerary vases, in which the ashes of the dead were placed, decorated with a scene of lamentation.

Clay models of horsemen, human masks, part of a chariot, bearded vase with a high neck.
Bronze tripod.

Case 147
Clay plaque with a relief figure of a goddess raising her arms, from **Kavousi.**
Bronze figurines, the outstanding one being the kithara-player.
Anthropomorphic vase from **Adromyloi Siteias.**

Case 148
Large terracotta figurines of the goddess with raised arms from the settlement at **Karphi Lasithiou**. On their heads they have diadems decorated with discs and birds. The cylindrical part is a rendering of the goddess's dress.
Clay model of a chariot with the driver, pulled by three oxen (only the heads are depicted), from **Karphi.**

Case 149
Finds from the cult cave of Eileithyia at Inatos (Tsoutsouros) in south Crete
Terracotta figurines placed in the cave as *ex votos*: models of couples making love, pregnant women, women feeding their babies, and a child in a cradle.
Terracotta dedications: models of a ship and a double axe.
Stone altar.
Small Egyptian figurines of glass paste and ivory.

Case 150
Finds from the cemeteries at Tekes Knossou
Cinerary urn.
Jugs, small cups, small kraters.

Case 151
Finds from the cemetery at Prinias (ancient Rizenia)
Stirrup-jars and other vases.
Terracotta figurines and models of a horse and birds.
Iron weapons and fibulae.
Gold jewellery in the shape of figure-of-eight shields with a swastika (symbol of the sun).

West wall
Pithoi with band, rope and herring-bone decoration, from **Dreros.**

Opposite page:
clay rhyton in the form of a chariot with its rider, drawn by three oxen.

Case 153
Finds from the cemetery at Fortetsa near Knossos
Iron weapons and tools.
Iron fibulae for fastening clothing.
Small clay model of a fish from **Berati Siteias.**

Case 154
Finds from the settlement at Karphi Lasithiou
Clay model of a shrine with an altar surmounted by horns, with small animals in the corners.
Candelabrum in the form of a bowl with a model of a goddess.
Tablet with a human figure.
Anthropomorphic rhyton.
Clay model of a horse.
Square model of a house or temple with a door.

Case 155
Finds from tombs at Knossos and Phaistos
Amphoras with decorative bands, maeander-patterns and other geometric motifs.
Amphora decorated with a horse and a star.

Case 156
Finds from the tomb at Tekes Knossou
Richly decorated krater and other vases.

Case 157
Finds from the tomb at Tekes Knossou
Cinerary urn decorated with rosettes, spirals and maeander-patterns.

Case 158
Finds from the cult cave of Eileithyia at Inatos (Tsoutsouros)
Necklaces, fibulae, pins – offerings to the goddess of child-birth.
Bone figurines of a naked goddess.
Gold discs and rosettes.
Bronze models of a double axe.
Egyptian scarabs.
Bone objects in the shape of a pipe, possibly used as handles of fans, or to wind thread.

Terracotta model of a house with a large round hole at the top, in which a vase was placed.

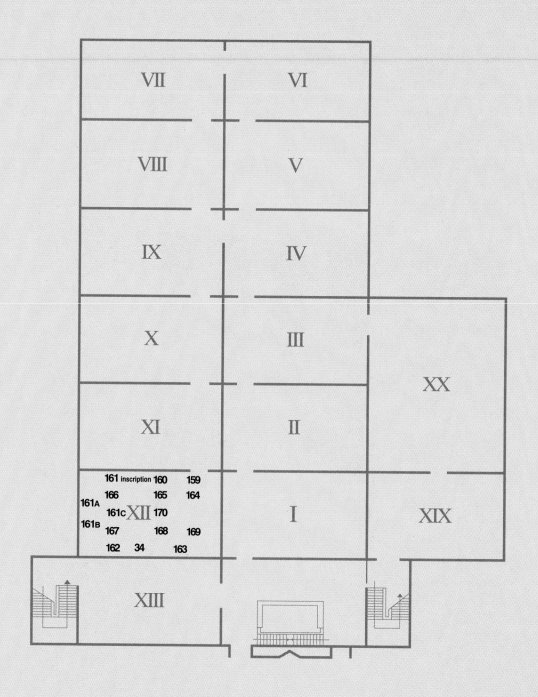

VII

VI

VIII

V

IX

IV

X

III

XX

XI

II

161 inscription 160   159
166   165   164
161A
161C XII 170
161B
167   168   169
162   34   163

I

XIX

XIII

ROOM XII

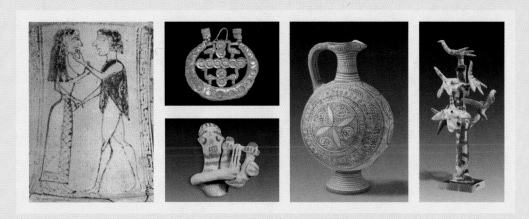

MATURE GEOMETRIC AND ORIENTALISING PERIODS (800 - 650 BC)

Finds from the cemeteries of the Geometric and the Orientalising or Early Archaic period at Fortetsa in the area of Knossos and Arkades (modoern Aphrati). Also, finds from the Idaean Cave, the sanctuary of Hermes and Aphrodite at Symi Viannou, dating from the Minoan period, the Iron Age, the Archaic period and the Hellenistic period.

They include: relief pithoi; large cinerary urns with scenes from mythology; other clay vases and vessels; bronze parts of a tripod with a scene from mythology; a gold cutout and gold band with divine figures; a bronze belt with relief decoration; and jewellery of gold, silver and other materials.

The votives from the sanctuary at Symi are rare finds: bronze cutouts depicting adorants with offerings; bronze and terracotta figurines; bronze swords; seals and other jewellery.

Right:
plastic vase in the form of a
tree with birds in its branches.

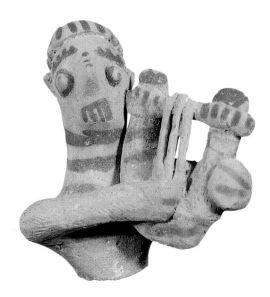

Part of a terracotta figurine of
a musician playing the lyre.

Depiction of a couple, detail
from the neck of an oinochoe.

Case 159
Fins from tombs at Fortetsa near Knossos
Polychrome pottery with blue and red paint on a white ground.
Krater decorated with a wild goat.
Cinerary urn with a depiction of a goddess with raised arms,
with a snake coiled around her.

Case 160
Finds from the sanctuary of Hermes and Aphrodite at Symi Viannou
The sanctuary was founded in the Minoan, Pre-palace period

(2000 BC) and continued in use until the end of antiquity.

From the Minoan period of the sanctuary:
Stone vases and altars, one with an incised Linear A inscription.
Bronze votive swords.
Bronze figurines of worshippers.
Clay tubular vessel (model of a trumpet?).
Clay vases with relief rings.

From the Early Iron Age:
Bronze figurines of naked ithyphallic male figures, a warrior with a spear, and a flute-player.
Terracotta figurines of worshippers.

On the wall
Inscription 'to Hermes Dendrites' dating from the 3rd c. AD.

Case 161
Finds dating from the Archaic and Hellenistic periods from the sanctuary of Hermes and Aphrodite at Symi Viannou
Bronze figurine of the god Hermes with a lyre.
Bronze figurine of an archer.
Bronze figurine of a centaur.
Bronze figurines of bulls, rams, goats and wild goats.
Terracotta and bronze figurines of human figures.
Stone altars.

Case 161A
Bronze cutouts dedicated in the sanctuary, with depictions of the god Hermes and worshippers offering animals on the sacred mountain.

Case 161B
Figurines of a naked goddess.
Small votive shields.
Silver pins.
Terracotta lamps.

Case 161Γ
Finds from the sanctuary of Hermes and Aphrodite at Symi Viannou
Minoan bronze votive swords.
Minoan seals.

Parts of bronze votive tripods.
Gold and silver jewellery and pieces of gold and silver sheet.

Case 162
Finds from tombs at Fortetsa near Knossos
Clay models of monkeys and other animals.
Clay model of a sacred tree with birds sitting on it.
Clay model of a ship with a passenger.
Small proto-Corinthian aryballoi.

Case 163
Finds from the cemetery at Arkades (Aphrati Pediadas)
Pottery in the Orientalising style.
Cinerary urn with a scene of a dead man and a mourning woman.
Jug with a trefoil mouth, from Rhodes.
Oinochoe with a scene of lovers, possibly Theseus and Ariadne.
Vases decorated with imaginary beings (sphinxes, winged horses, lions).
Clay models of an owl, a sitting lion, a seated mourner and a lyre-player.

Case 164
Finds from tombs at Fortetsa near Knossos
Bronze votive belt with repoussé decoration of a shrine and a trinity of deities, being attacked from war chariots and defended by archers.
Sherds of vases with depictions of an octopus, a sphinx and human figures.

Case 165
Finds from tombs at Fortetsa near Knossos
Cinerary urns with lids, with polychrome decoration.
Small vase in the shape of a duck.

Clay oinochoe with Orientalising decoration.

Two-handled vase decorated with a depiction of a goddess holding branches between two aquatic birds.

Case 166
Finds from tombs at Fortetsa near Knossos
Cinerary urns with monochrome decoration of geometric motifs, bands, chevrons, concentric circles, guilloches, maeanders and stylised birds and trees. White paint is used very occasionally.

Case 167
Finds from tombs at Fortetsa near Knossos
Polychrome cinerary urns decorated with rows of leaves, palmettes, guilloches, stylised trees, birds, etc.
Small cinerary urn with a scene of a man and woman. The male figure wears a helmet and is perhaps Theseus, with the female being Ariadne, or the scene may depict two gods.

Case 168
Finds from the cemetery at Arkades (Aphrati Pediadas)
Cinerary urns decorated with geometric motifs, circles, mae-anders, etc.
Vases in the orientalising style decorated with sphinxes, griffins, lion's heads, confronted lions with a shared head.
Clay and bronze vases containing the burned bones of the dead and a small aryballos.
Cylindrical cinerary urn with a lid, with a scene of a male figure leading a horse.
Cinerary urn with a winged figure (possibly Talos) between two sphinxes.
Two-handled vase with a scene of the goddess of vegetation holding sacred trees in her hands, between aquatic birds.

Case 169
Bronze objects from the decoration of tripod cauldrons found in the **Idaean Cave**. A man and woman travel in a ship with a row of oarsmen; the man is armed, wears a helmet and carries a shield, and the woman raises her arms. This is the abduction of a goddess, or the abduction of Ariadne by Theseus. A large bird carries off a sailor. The decoration also includes chariots, warriors, women with animals, sphinxes, etc.
Bronze sheathing for a quiver with repoussé representations of the Lord of the Animals between alternating lions and sphinxes.
Small votive greaves from **Kavousi.**
Pierced metal sheet, possibly depicting the mythical figure of winged Talos.

Case 170
Finds from the tomb at Tekes Knossou
Necklace of gold and rock crystal in the shape of a crescent from which suns and crescent moons are suspended by gold chains.
Gold ornament with a cross in a crescent, ending in human heads. There are gold birds in the gaps.
Necklace with beads of rock crystal.
Gold band with a repeated depiction of the Lord of the Animals holding lions.
Gold figures of men carrying sheep on their shoulders.
Delicate gold chains with silver pins for the hair.
Piece of gold sheet from the **Idaean Cave** with a depiction of a goddess between two male attendants (possibly Helen and the Dioskouroi).

Gold pendant in the shape of a crescent moon ending in human heads.
At the centre is a cross-shaped ornament and four aquatic birds.

Gold bead in the shape of a lion's head.
Ivory scarab.
Gold jewellery from the tomb at **Rotasi (ancient Rytion)**.

East wall
Large pithoi with relief decoration of sphinxes, rosettes, shields, spirals and leaves from ancient **Lyttos** (Xeidas).

West wall
Relief pithoi from **Arkades** (Aphrati), decorated with spirals terminating in lion's heads, rosettes, small embossed shields, maeanders, palmettes and networks of spirals.

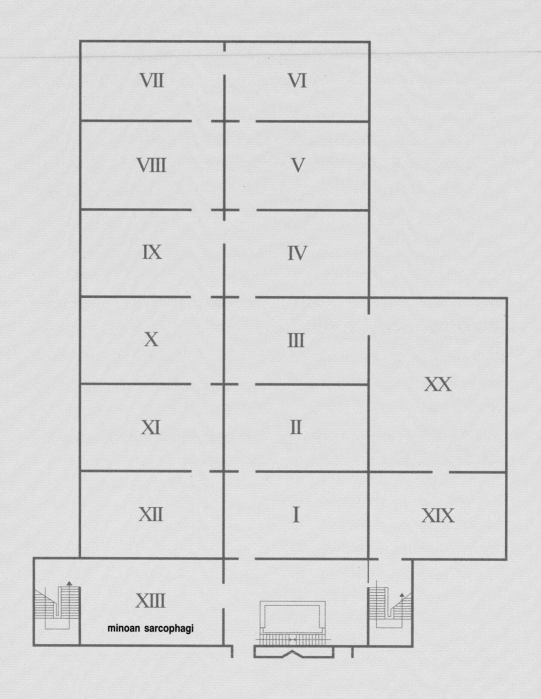

VII

VI

VIII

V

IX

IV

X

III

XX

XI

II

XII

I

XIX

XIII

minoan sarcophagi

ROOM XIII

MINOAN SARCOPHAGI

This room contains typical sarcophagi in which the dead were buried. There are three basic shapes: cist-shaped with a pyramidal or saddle lid, elliptical, and bathtub-shaped. Some of the sarcophagi are decorated with cult scenes and cult symbols.

Room XIII is devoted to the display of a selection of sarcophagi dating from the last centuries of the Minoan period (15th-12th c. BC).

Detail of the decoration of the sarcophagus on this page, showing aquatic birds and fish.

Cist-shaped sarcophagus with a pitched lid.
The decoration is of stylised papyrus flowers, aquatic birds, and fish.

The custom of burying the dead in clay coffins had its beginnings in Pre-palace times and continued on into the Old Palace period. It appears, however, that most of the sarcophagi were made of wood and have not been preserved. The later cist-shaped sarcophagi are imitations of wooden ones.
The earliest surviving sarcophagi are oval in shape.
The sarcophagi on display in this room belong to two basic types: the bathtub-shaped and the cist-shaped, which usually had a saddle lid. They are short, but this does not imply that the dead interred in them were not tall, since they were placed in a contracted position. The skeletons in the north-east corner (from Archanes and Sellopoulo) show the burial position.

Cist-shaped sarcophagus with decoration of a boat and aquatic birds.

The bathtub-shaped sarcophagi were decorated both inside and out, and the cist-shaped on the outer sides and lid; the motifs were drawn from the pottery of the time, and were usually geometric designs, stylised flowers, palm trees, papyrus plants, octopuses, fish, bovines, wild goats and birds.

Some sarcophagi were decorated with scenes connected with burial cult or the worship of the deity, or render the Minoan paradise. A sarcophagus from Milatos has a hieratic figure with raised arms, and one from Palaikastro is decorated with horns of consecration and griffins. Another from Athanatoi has cult symbols and one from Kalochoraphitis in Mesara has bucrania, ships, argonauts, animals, birds, fish and a chariot.

Bathtub-shaped sarcophagus, the inside decorated with fish and the outside with scale pattern, discs, and "triglyphs".

Detail of the decoration of the sarcophagus on this page, showing a wild goat suckling her young.

Bathtub-shaped sarcophagus decorated with wild goats.

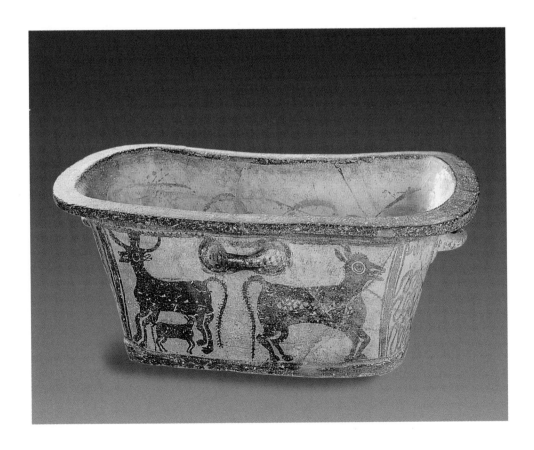

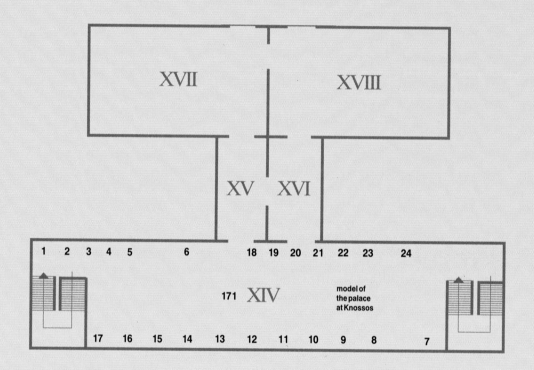

XVII

XVIII

XV XVI

1 2 3 4 5 6   18 19 20 21 22 23 24

171 XIV   model of
the palace
at Knossos

17 16 15 14 13 12 11 10 9 8 7

ROOM XIV

Minoan Wall-paintings

In the centre of this room is displayed the famous painted stone sarcophagus from Ayia Triada, with scenes of sacrifice and cult.

The wall-paintings displayed on the walls come from the palaces at Knossos and Ayia Triada, and from the villa at Amnisos. They include the wall-paintings with the procession, the bull-leaper, and the griffin, the relief priest-king, and the relief bull, and wall-paintings depicting landscapes and hunting scenes, partridges, lilies and octopuses.

At the east end of the room is displayed a wooden reconstruction of the palace of Knossos.

The west side of the famous stone (poros) Ayia Triada sarcophagus. In the centre of the fresco, against a white background, is a depiction of a bull being sacrificed to the accompaniment of a flute. The blood of the sacrificial animal is collected in a bucket. At the left, against a yellow background, a priestess places her hands on the sacrificial victim, and there is a procession of women behind her.
At the right, against a dark background, another priestess, wearing a sheepskin, offers a bloodless sacrifice on the altar in front of the sanctuary.
A black bird is depicted on a double axe.

Detail of a decorative zone of the sarcophagus containing linked spirals with rosettes at the centre.

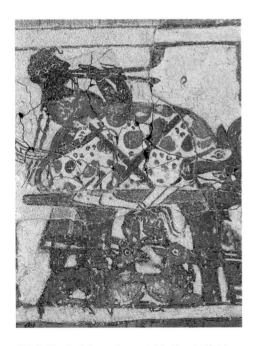

Detail of the depiction on the west side. The sacrificial bull on the table.
At the back is the flute-player, and there are wild goats sitting under the table.

Detail of the depiction on the west side. The priestess offers a bloodless sacrifice on an altar. A libation jug and a basket of fruit are shown.
Behind the altar is a double axe on a column, with a black bird sitting on it.
At the right is the facade of the sanctuary with double horns and the sacred tree.

Case 171
The Ayia Triada sarcophagus

One of the finest monuments of Minoan art is displayed in the centre of the large picture gallery on the first floor of the Museum. It is a stone (poros) cist-shaped sarcophagus completely covered with painted plaster. It was found in a tomb next to the palace at Ayia Triada, and was probably used for a royal burial. It dates from the period of the third palaces in the 14th c. BC. The painted decoration of the sarcophagus includes scenes of the worship of the deity and the cult of the dead.

The east side of the sarcophagus.
At the left, against a white background, a priestess pours the blood of the sacrificial victim into a krater from a container, while behind her another priestess carries two buckets, followed by a musician playing a lyre.
At the centre, three men wearing sheepskins offer animals and a model of a ship to a male figure –possibly the dead man– standing between a building and a tree.

Detail of the depiction on the east side.
The priestess unconcernedly empties a container
into a krater set between two double axes, on
each of which sits a black bird.

Detail of the depiction on the east side.
A man offers a model of a ship to a figure standing
between a tree and a building.

The left part of the depiction on the east side. A priestess pours what may be the blood of the
sacrificial victim from a container into a krater, while another priestess behind her carries two
buckets, followed by a musician playing the seven-stringed lyre.

Wall-paintings

Wall-paintings were the large-scale art of the Minoans. For about five centuries (1800-1300 BC) they adorned the interiors of the Minoan palaces and megara. The extensively restored wall-paintings on display in the Herakleion Museum decorated the palaces and megara of Knossos, the palace of

The Ayia Triada sarcophagus:
the depiction on the north end.
At the bottom is a chariot with two goddesses, drawn by wild goats, with a procession of men at the top.

Ayia Triada, and the megara of Amnisos, Tylissos and Pseira. Recent excavations have shown that other palaces and megara were also adorned with wall-paintings (Archanes and Galatas). The first wall-paintings on display (nos. 1-15) are from the palace at Knossos, followed by those from Amnisos (16, 17) and those from Ayia Triada (18-24).

The Ayia Triada sarcophagus:
the depiction on the south end.
A chariot with two goddesses, drawn by winged griffins, with a bird flying above them.

North wall (west part)

Wall-painting with the leg of a bull (1). The bull was depicted larger than life size. It dates from the final phase of the palace at Knossos, c. 1400 BC.

Wall-painting of the procession (2-5). This painting, which is preserved in a very fragmentary condition, adorned the corridor named after it in the west and south part of the palace at Knossos. It dates from the 14th c. BC (final phase of the palace). Of the roughly 250 figures it is reckoned to have contained, all that survive are the legs of a few figures and the head of a male figure, and most of the famous rhyton-bearer (3). The small-scale reconstruction gives an idea of part of the procession. In the centre is depicted a female figure with her arms raised, perhaps a queen or princess acting the part of the goddess, dressed in white clothing with white skin.

Wall-painting of a griffin (6). This comes from the throne room in the west wing of the final palace at Knossos, where the royal throne was protected by two confronted seated griffins (an imaginary beast with the head of a bird and body of a lion) set amongst plants.

The relief wall-painting of the bull.

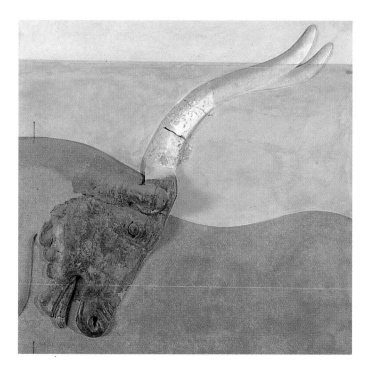

South wall

Wall-painting of shields (7). East end of the south wall. This adorned the portico of the Grand Staircase that led to the royal apartments in the final palace. The coloured blobs render the sewn animal hides used to make the shields.

Relief wall-painting of the lily prince (8). This relief, assembled from a large number of pieces and restored, depicts a youth (possibly a prince or high-priest), wearing a loincloth and a codpiece, a necklace of lilies, and a crown of peacock's feathers and lilies on his head. This restoration has recently been disputed.

Relief wall-painting of a bull (9). Only the head of the animal, full of vigour, agony and power, is preserved. The scene of the capture of a bull adorned the balcony at the north entrance of the palace. It is dated to about 1600 BC.

Ladies in Blue wall-painting (10). This adorned the antechamber of the large throne room in the east wing of the **palace at Knossos**. The ladies, elegantly dressed and bedecked in Minoan fashion, are chatting to each other.

Wall-painting of dolphins (11). This adorned the Queen's Megaron in the palace at Knossos. "Dolphins and fish swim in the brilliant network created by the sun's rays on the sandy bottom of the sea and in the waves" (St. Alexiou).

Wall-painting of spirals (12-13). Zones with polychrome spirals, from the east wing of the **palace at Knossos**.

The figure of the rhyton-bearer from the large wall-painting of the procession.

Opposite page: the wall-painting of the dolphins.

Wall-painting of partridges (14). This decorated a frieze in the Caravan-Serai to the south of the **palace at Knossos**. The partridges, of a species still found in Crete, move in a rocky landscape with scant vegetation. Amongst them is a hoopoe.

Wall-painting of bull-leapers (15). This adorned a room in the east wing of the **palace at Knossos**. The bull is depicted in a flying gallop. An acrobat is executing the dangerous leap over its back. A second figure holds the bull by the horns and a third stands behind it.

Wall-painting of lilies (16, 17). This comes from the villa of the same name at **Amnisos**. White lilies and red irises spring between structures in front of a stepped border.

North wall (east part, from the left)

Wall-painting of a kneeling woman (18). A richly attired female figure kneels amongst plants. The wall-painting is blackened by the fire that destroyed the palace.

Wall-painting of a woman at a shrine (19). Blackened, like the previous painting, this depicts a female figure in colourful dress next to a shrine with double horns.

The wall-painting with the partridges.

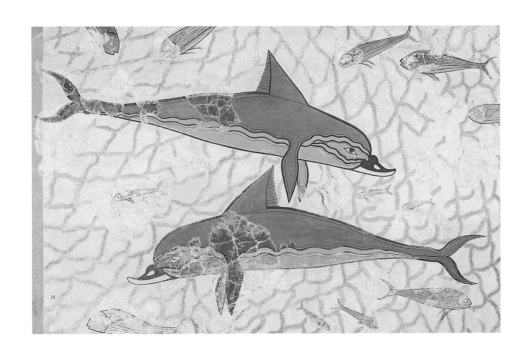

Wall-painting of a wildcat (20). Better preserved than the others, this depicts a verdant landscape in which wildcats hunt birds (pheasants, hoopoes etc.). One of the wildcats is shown with a rapacious look in its eye and its body stretched in an arc.

Wall-painting with a procession of men and women (21). This depicts a musician with a seven-string lyre, a flute-player and priests and priestesses carrying buckets. The scene recalls that on the Ayia Triada sarcophagus.

Wall-painting with a procession of women (22). This depicts a procession of female worshippers in two rows. There are small colonnettes amongst them.

Wall-painting of an animal sacrifice (23). This wall-painting depicts a woman leading a deer to an altar.

Painted floor with a seascape (24). This adorned the shrine at Ayia Triada in the 14th c. BC. It depicts octopuses, dolphins and fish.

The "ladies in blue" wall-painting.

The wall-painting of the lilies.

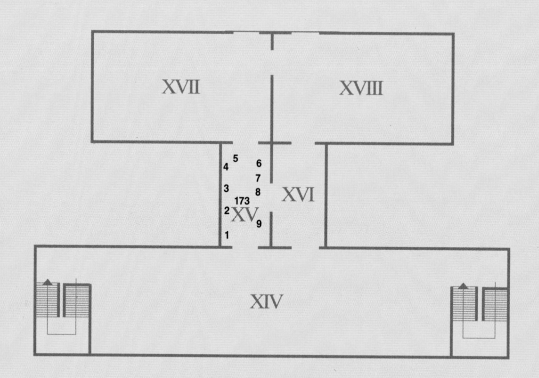

ROOM XV

MINOAN WALL-PAINTINGS

This room contains: the miniature wall-paintings of the sacred grove and the tripartite shrine, the figure of "la Parisienne", and the fragments of relief figures, all from Knossos. In the flat case are displayed fragments of wall-paintings from Knossos and Tylisos.

West wall (from the left)
Wall-painting of a sacred grove (1). Miniature fresco from the apartments on the upper floor of the west wing of the palace at Knossos. Women with white skin and men with red skin set in a landscape beneath trees, watch a performance of women dancing, possibly in the west courtyard of the palace.

Wall-painting of a tripartite shrine (2). The tripartite shrine in the central courtyard of the palace is depicted at the centre of the painting. To right and left, women or priestesses wearing impressive dress sit or stand on balconies or staircases.

Wall-painting of "la Parisienne", and the libation wall-painting (3, 4). "La Parisienne", with her large eyes, curly hair, bright red lips and turned-up nose, is part of a composition in which male and female hieratic figures, seated on stools, are offered libations from communion cups.

On the **north wall** is displayed part of a **relief painted ceiling** consisting of spirals and yellow rosettes.

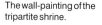

The wall-painting of the tripartite shrine.

On the **east wall** are displayed pieces of large relief paintings **(6, 7, 8)**, depicting athletes and relief griffins tied to columns.

Case 173

Fragments of wall-paintings from **Knossos** and **Tylissos**. One piece from Knossos has a diagrammatic representation of the **labyrinth (69)**, another depicts a **piece of cloth (29)**, and a third the **tail of a bird (37)**. Pieces from Tylissos have a miniature rendering of **men and women (87, 89, 90)**.

On the east side of the case is a fragment (36) with a relief representation of fingers holding a necklace from which amulets are suspended. A fragment of wall-painting preserves the wings of a bird and another depicts the head of a feline, while other pieces depict sphinxes, male figures and flowers.

The wall-painting of "la Parisienne".

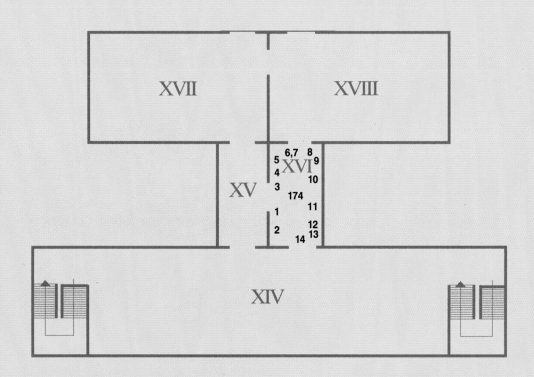

ROOM XVI

MINOAN WALL-PAINTINGS

Relief wall-painting
depicting olives.

The finds here include: the wall-painting of the saffron-gatherer monkey, the dancing-girl, the bluebird from Knossos, the relief wall-painting with parts of the human body from Pseira, and the sacral knot from the megaron at Nirou.

In the flat case are displayed fragments of wall-paintings from Knossos with various motifs.

The following wall-paintings are displayed on the **west wall:**
Wall-painting of the saffron-gatherer monkey (1). This comes from the north-west part of the **palace at Knossos**. It depicts a blue monkey gathering saffron flowers. The figure was formerly interpreted as a boy **(2)**.
Wall-painting of the captain of the blacks (3). This depicts an officer leading a group of black soldiers.
Wall-painting of the dancing girl (4). This comes from the **Queen's Megaron** in the palace at Knossos. It has recently been restored as a figure receiving a report.
Wall-painting of the tricolumnar shrine (5). The columns of the shrine have double axes fixed to them.

On the **north wall** are displayed relief wall-paintings depicting olive trees **(6-8)**.

The wall-painting of the saffron-gatherer (old restoration)

Right:
The relief wall-painting of the seated goddess from Pseira.

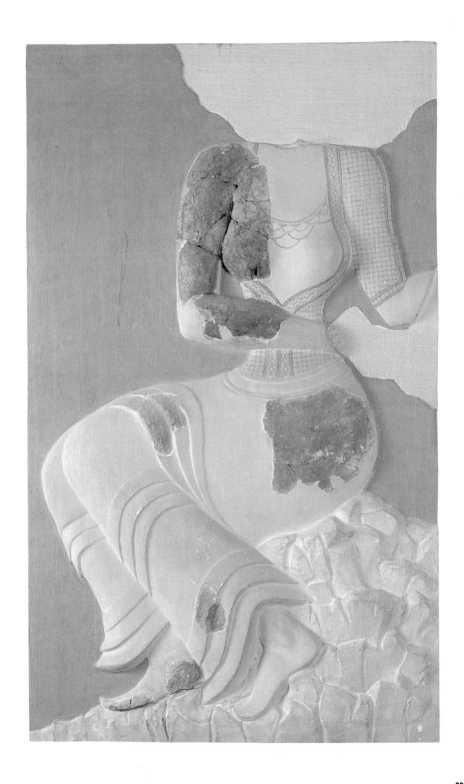

The bluebird fresco

The **east wall** has wall-paintings from the House of the Frescoes at Knossos, including the **bluebird fresco (9)** and the **wall-painting with monkeys (10-11)**, which are shown amidst rocks and wild flowers.
Relief wall-paintings with arms, legs and parts of human figures, from the megara in the **harbour town of Pseira (12-13)**.

On the **south wall** is the **wall-painting of the sacral knot (14)**, from the Minoan **megaron at Nirou.**

Case 174
Small fragments of wall-paintings.
Wall-painting of the palanquin (59), preserved in fragmentary condition. A priest or priestess in a litter.
Miniature wall-painting of a crowd of men (58) and part of a **wall-painting with the head of an animal (57)**.
Part of a wall-painting with a **woman bull-leaper (34)**, wearing gold jewellery.
Fragments of miniature wall-paintings **(66, 67, 70)**, showing

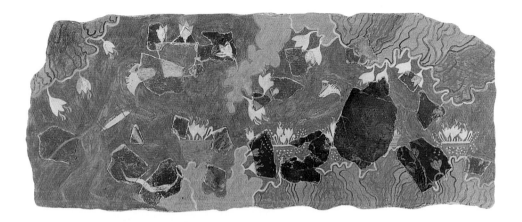

The wall-painting of the saffron-gatherer monkey.

Detail of the wall-painting with the blue monkeys.

richly dressed women and men in animated conversation.
Fragment of a wall-painting with a depiction of a bull's head
(51)
Fragment of a wall-painting with a composition of sphinxes set
in a pediment, with a bucranium at the centre.

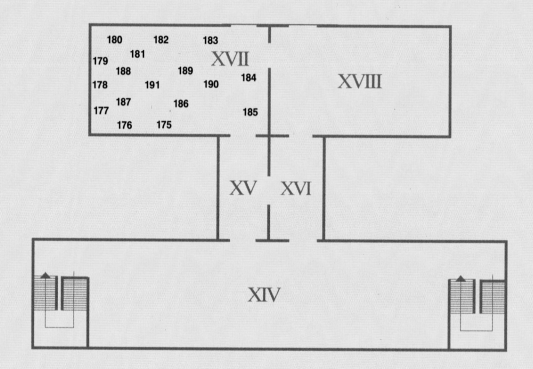

ROOM XVII

GIAMALAKIS COLLECTION

The most important exhibits in the Collection are the Neolithic terracotta figurine of the "fertility goddess" from Ierapetra; the clay model of a small temple from Archanes; the hoard of gold objects from Zakros; sealstones and Oriental cylinder seals; bronze tools and weapons; gold jewellery; and coins of various cities.

In 1962, the collection of Stylianos Giamalakis, a doctor in Herakleion and lover of the ancient world, was purchased for the Herakleion Museum.

Case 175
Neolithic terracotta figurine of a seated female figure representing the fertility goddess, as is clear from the rendering of her as steatopygous. Found at Kato Chorio near Ierapetra.
Clay and stone vases and vessels of unknown provenance, dating from Pre-palace times.
Triple kernos consisting of vases in the shape of birds (unknown provenance).
Frying-pan vessel and stone vases from the Cyclades.

Case 176
Stone nest-shaped vases.
Bronze cult axes.
Stone altars and lamps.
Clay rhyton.
Bronze and terracotta figurines of the Old Palace period.
Top shelf: stone and clay vases of the Old Palace period, of unknown provenance.

Case 177
Jugs, stirrup-jars, alabastra and three-handled vases from the second and final palace phases (unknown provenance).

Case 178
Bronze figurine of a man carrying a ram on his shoulders, for sacrifice.

Terracotta figurine of a seated goddess of the Neolithic period.

Case 179

Terracotta "wing-shaped" figurines with raised arms, figurines of bulls, and vases of Mycenaean origins.
Heads and parts of figurines of the goddess with raised arms, dating from the Late Minoan period.
Double cult vase with a human figure in an attitude of worship.
Kraters of Late Minoan (Post-palace) date.

Case 180

Bottom shelf: clay vases of Protogeometric date, possibly from a tomb at **Archanes.**
Protogeometric vases.

Case 181

Painted terracotta model of a small shrine, from **Archanes**. Through the doorway can be seen a terracotta figurine of the goddess with raised arms. The doorway was closed by a wooden door. Two male figures stretched out on the roof look at the figurine of the goddess through the opening. The dog that guarded the shrine is lying on the roof. The model dates from the Protogeometric period.

Case 182

Clay vases of the Archaic and Classical periods from Boeotian, Attic and Corinthian workshops.
Heads of terracotta figurines from **Axos.**
Bronze figurine of a goddess riding on a lion.

Case 183

Gold, silver and bronze coins from Cretan and other Greek cities, some dating from Roman times and some being more recent European coins.

Case 184

Marble heads of Roman times.
Figurines of worshippers and a seated goddess dating from the Hellenistic period.
Attic black-figure vases.
Bronze vessels.
Hellenistic pottery.

Case 185

Glass vases in a variety of shapes.
Terracotta and bronze figurines of Roman times.

Clay vases of the 4th and 3rd c. BC.

Case 186
Bronze tools and weapons: swords, spears, daggers, bronze double axes, saws, leather-cutters, and small scrapers, dating from Minoan times.
Ivory figurines of the Pre-palace period.
Marble Cycladic figurines of the Pre-palace period.
Ivory seal in the form of a monkey.

Case 187
Seals dating from the Pre-palace and New Palace periods, made of semiprecious stones: sardius, sardonyx, steatite, jasper, haematite, amethyst and agate. They are engraved with hieroglyphs and depictions of animals and plants.

Case 189
Eastern (Babylonian) cylinders with depictions of deities, daemons and mythical animals.
Seals of the Persian Sassanid dynasty (3rd-7th c. AD).

Case 189
Parts of relief pithoi dating from the Archaic period. They have scenes of sphinxes, horses, lions and chariot-races.
Bronze "girdle" used to protect the soldier's belly, with the name of the owner, Phrixos, inscribed in an archaic Cretan alphabet.
Bronze mirrors, pins, arrowheads and a fibula.
Child's doll with moving limbs, and Archaic figurines.
Moulds for making figurines.

Case 190
Bronze Corinthian-type helmet from **Axos**. The cheekpieces protected the cheeks and the vertical section the nose.

Case 191
East side: gold jewellery from Zakros
Bull's head with a rosette of connected spirals on the forehead.
Diadem with a depiction of the Mistress of the Animals taming two wild goats.
Bowl with relief decoration of connected spirals.

Other sides: jewellery of various periods
Gold earrings decorated in the granulation technique, in the

form of wild goats and doves.

Bronze finger-ring with an ivory bezel and a depiction of a sphinx.

Apotropaic gorgoneion (mask of a grimacing Medusa).

Gold earrings with glass-paste beads.

Finger-ring with a scene of courting birds.

Sheet of metal with a depiction of Leda.

Large finger-ring with a depiction of a small Eros on a lion.

Necklace and earrings with rubies and pearls, dating from the Venetian occupation of the island.

To the right of the north entrance

Relief with a scene of the Idaean Cave.

Terracotta model of a circular temple.

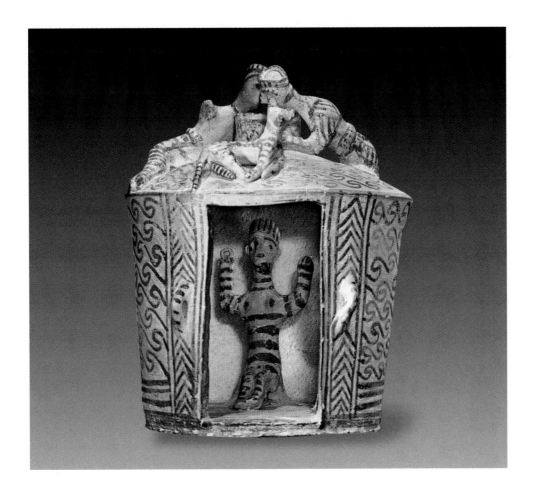

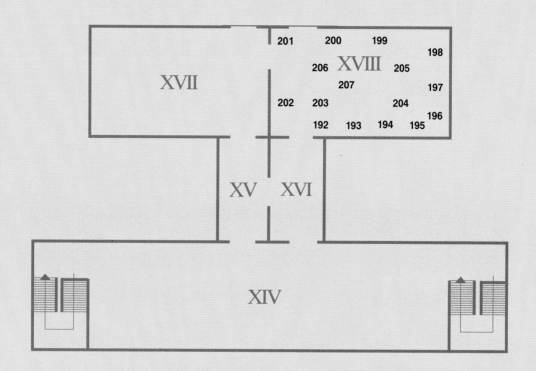

XVII

201 200 199
        198
206 XVIII 205
  207
        197
202 203   204
        196
192 193 194 195

XV XVI

XIV

ROOM XVIII

Minor Arts of Archaic, Classical, Hellenistic and Roman Times (7th. c. BC - 4th c. AD)

In this room are displayed finds from various sites, dating from the Iron Age to the end of antiquity, from Ierapetra, Gortyn, Axos, Praisos, Arkades, the Idaean and Diktaean Caves, Asites, Vatheia, Kounavi, Malia, and other sites.

They include: a bronze statue of a youth; terracotta figurines; a terracotta statue of Athena; bronze figurines of men, women and animals; a bronze breastplate and bronze moulds; clay vessels; gold jewellery; and coins from the Cretan cities.

Case 192
Finds from the Archaic shrine deposit at Gortyn
Terracotta figurines depicting the goddess Athena.
Terracotta figurines of horses.
Stone and bronze figurines.
Clay vases of the Orientalising period.
Small votive terracotta shields.

Case 193
Finds from the Archaic shrine deposit at Gortyn
Terracotta figurine of the goddess Athena wearing a helmet.

Case 194
Finds from the Archaic shrine deposit at Gortyn
Cult vessels: kernoi for multiple offerings of wheat, pulses, liquids etc.
Stone model of a shrine and part of a female figurine.
Black-figure dinos-krater with depictions of horse-races, wild goats, lions and birds.

Case 195
Finds from Praisos and Arkades
Terracotta figurines of men and women and an anthropomorphic vase (Arkades).
Parts of figurines, a seated goddess and a male figurine.
Gorgoneion and lamp with a nozzle in the form of a human head.
Clay dish with a depiction of a hero riding a sea monster (Praisos).

Jug with trefoil mouth and wild goats, from Rhodes.
Parts of relief pithoi with sphinxes.
Relief depicting an athlete's leg.

Case 196
Bronze figures of wild goats, oxen, lions, birds and snakes from
Amnisos and **the Psychro** and **Idaean Caves.**
Two bronze and one bone flute and an ancient "girdle" from
Arkades, inscribed with the owner's name: Okalanos.
Moulds and masks for figurines.
Legs of tripod cauldrons and wheels from the **Idaean Cave.**

Case 197
Bronze breastplate of a child or youth, from **Arkades.**

Case 198
Bronze vessels from the Geometric tombs at **Fortetsa**, and
from the **Idaean Cave.**
Helmet with relief winged horses from **Axos.**

Corners of the east wall
Pithoi with relief scenes of sphinxes, from **Kato Vathia.**

Case 199
Imported Attic black- and red-figure pottery
Red-figure pelike with a scene of the Arimaspeans and griffins.
Vase with a scene of Dionysos and a Maenad.
Lekythos with a scene of women offering a libation (from Ky-
donia).
Bell kraters with depictions of nymphs, satyrs and Dionysiac
scenes.
Back-figure lekythos depicting Theseus and the Minotaur.
Boeotian and Corinthian vases made available by the National
Archaeological Museum in Athens.

Case 200
Deposit in the sanctuary of Demeter at Gortyn
Large lamps with many nozzles for wicks, used in mystery rituals.
Terracotta figurines of worshippers holding young pigs (the
sacred animal of Demeter).
Terracotta figurines of women with the sacred kiste on
their head, with the vessels for the mysteries, and wearing
wreaths on their bodies.

Terracotta figurine of the
goddess Athena.

Silver coin with the head of Minos on one side and the labyrinth on the other.

Figurines of Demeter, depicted grieving for the death of Persephone.

Clay baskets of Hellenistic date, from **Knossos**.

To right and left of case 200

Large panathenaic amphoras dating from the 4th c. BC. These were prizes for the victors in athletic competitions.

Case 201

Finds from the Hellenistic tomb at Gortyn

Winged figures of Eros.

Models of ostrich eggs.

Relief 'wedding' cauldron.

Glass vase.

Clay votive plaques from the shrine of the hero Hippeus at ancient **Eltynia** (Kounavi).

North-west corner of the room

Bronze funerary statue of a youth wearing a himation, from Ierapetra, 1st c. BC. The eyes were made of some other material and inlaid. The personal facial features and morose expression are accurately rendered. Fine portrait.

Silver coin with a depiction of the Minotaur.

Case 202

Glass vases from tombs of Roman date, found at **Herakleion**, **Knossos** and **Sokara**.
Bronze figurines of Roman date, from various sites.
Marble heads of Roman date.
Terracotta lamps with overtly erotic scenes.

Case 203

Bronze "girdle" that protected the belly of the soldier, with incised scenes of athletes competing for prizes.
Bronze bowl with scenes of sphinxes.
Bronze sheet with a depiction of Athena, from **Dreros**.
Handles of bronze cauldrons from the **Idaean Cave**.
Terracotta votive models of weapons and shields from the sanctuaries at **Gortyn** and **Praisos.**

Case 204

Ring-stones of Roman date with depictions of deities and humans.
Ring-stones with the inscription: *GREAT [IS] THE NAME OF SARAPIS.*
Persian seals of the Sassanid dynasty (3rd-7th c. AD), and an eastern cylinder seal.

Case 205
Coins of the Cretan cities
They depict the patron deity or hero of the city and its symbol.
The coins are from the following cities:
Aptera in Kydonia (with the hero Kydon the archer). **Polyrrhenia** (with a bull's head). **Phalasarna, Hyrtakina, Lissos, Modea** (with a bull's head), and **Elyros.**
Lappa, Axos and **Eleutherna.**
Knossos (with the Minotaur and labyrinth), **Phaistos** (with a depiction of Herakles with his club and bow, or with Talos and a bull's head), **Lyttos** (with an eagle or wild boar), **Priansos** and **Raukos**.
Hierapetra, Itanos (with a depiction of an anthropomorphic Triton), **Praisos** and the **Cretan League.**

Coins of other Greek cities with which the Cretan cities enjoyed relations
Athens, Megara, Corinth, Aegina, the Achaean League, Argos, Lacedaimon and Messenia.
The Macedonians (gold coins issued by Philip II and Cas-

sander), the Aegean islands, and cities in Asia Minor and Egypt.

Case 206
Finds from the Archaic shrine deposit on the acropolis of Gortyn
Terracotta figurines of a naked goddess of love and fertility. Made with a mould. The goddess is shown wearing a polos on her head and long tresses, with one hand on her breast and the other on the pudenda. She is also depicted seated on a throne with offerings in her hands.
Small terracotta shrine with a trinity of naked deities.
Terracotta plaques with depictions of sphinxes and the goddess placing a wreath on her head.
Terracotta plaques with a winged male figure amongst griffins and mythical scenes of the hero Bellerophon, the murder of Aigisthos, and Apollo playing the kithara.
Figurines and plaques of Hellenistic date. they depict Athena with her shield, a naked warrior, etc.

Case 207
Jewellery of Hellenistic and Roman times
Necklace, earrings and a pin from **Asites** near Herakleion.
Gold diadems with scenes of Artemis amongst deer, and lions chasing deer (unknown provenance).
Model of a bird carrying its young on its back, from **Knossos.**
Finger-rings with ring-stones from various sites.
Finger-ring with an "heirloom stone" with a depiction of a satyr's head, from **Knossos.**
Gold earrings, necklaces, pins and finger-rings from the Roman sarcophagus from **Malia.**

Case 207A
Bronze "girdles" with repoussé scenes of winged horses, from **Axos** (early 6th c. BC).
Parts of bronze votive shields with scenes of lions and bulls, from the **Idaean Cave** (8th-7th c. BC).
Bronze discs decorated with spirals, maeander pattern and palmettes, dating from the Hellenistic period, of unknown provenance.
Key and belt buckles of Roman date.
Bronze lion's head from a shield, and the base of a vase, from the **Idaean Cave.**
Bronze votive models of breastplates, helmets and "girdles", from an Archaic sanctuary at **Praisos.**

Detail showing the head of the statue.

Bronze statue of a youth.

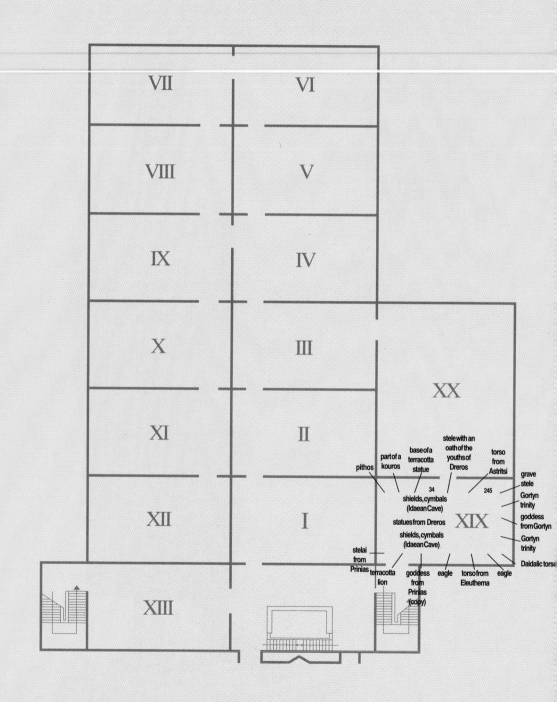

VII

VI

VIII

V

IX

IV

X

III

XX

XI

II

pithos

part of a
kouros

base of a
terracotta
statue

stele with an
oath of the
youths of
Dreros

torso
from
Astritsi

grave
stele

34

245

XII

I

shields, cymbals
(Idaean Cave)

Gortyn
trinity

statues from Dreros

goddess
from Gortyn

shields, cymbals
(Idaean Cave)

XIX

Gortyn
trinity

stelai
from
Prinias

Daidalic torso

terracotta
lion

goddess
from
Prinias
(copy)

eagle

torso from
Eleutherna

eagle

XIII

ROOM XIX

MONUMENTAL ART OF THE ARCHAIC PERIOD

Relief bull from the neck of an Archaic pithos from Phaistos.

The monumental art that evolved in Crete in the 7th and 6th centuries BC produced some unique works. They come from Prinias, Gortyn, Phaistos, Arkades, Dreros, the Idaean Cave, Amnisos, Eleutherna, Astritsi, Palaikastro, Axos, Kounavi and Ierapetra. They include: architectural reliefs of a horseman; a trinity of deities; a terracotta sima with lion's heads; statues of the seated goddess; torsoes of kouroi; statues of an eagle and a hawk; relief pithoi; grave stelai; bronze hammered statues; bronze cymbals and bronze shields; and the stele inscribed with the hymn to Zeus.

Monumental sculpture flourished in Crete in the 7th and 6th c. BC, producing relief and sculptural architectural decoration and free-standing sculptures, made of poros or clay. At the same time, there was a flowering of metal-working which also created monumental works of art, such as hammered statues and large shields with relief decoration. This room also houses some engraved funerary stelai, inscriptions, and pithoi with relief decoration. Our visit begins at the west, to the visitor's left, and continues to the north, then to the centre and finally to the south and east.

West wall
The frieze from the temple at Prinias (ancient Rizenia)
The large poros slabs are carved in relief with a procession of horsemen carrying shields and spears. The position occupied by the frieze on the temple was probably above the entrance to the prodomos (see the drawing on the north wall). It dates from the 7th c. BC.

Above the entrance in the north wall
The lintel of the entrance to the temple at Prinias
The monumental portal was placed at the entrance to the cella in the temple at Prinias. Two goddesses carved in poros sit above the lintel. Wild animals are depicted on their dress. On the front of the lintel are relief lions and deer. The goddess is also carved in relief on the underside of the lintel. The temple belonged to the Mistress of the Animals, possibly Rhea.

The torso of the statue from Eleutherna.

Bronze cymbal from the
Idaean Cave.

West side

In the centre of this side is the preserved lower part of a poros
cult statue of the goddess, found in the **Archaic temple on the
acropolis at Gortyn.** The goddess is depicted seated and her
dress is decorated with rosettes, palmettes and spirals.

Either side of the seated goddess are two large architectural
reliefs from the same temple depicting a trinity of deities. In
the first relief the god is shown in the centre moving to the left,
embracing the two goddesses, who are naked and wear only
the polos, the divine head-cover, on their head. The other relief depicts three similar naked figures of gods who also wear
the polos.

Two Archaic grave stelai depict a female figure with a distaff and a warrior with a shield, both in a double border. They come from the **acropolis at Prinias.**
Flower-shaped column capital with a rectangular abacus decorated with a spiral, from **Arkades.**
Poros lion's head from **Phaistos.**
Poros gorgoneion from **Dreros**, 7th c. BC.

North side
The upper part of a funerary statue of poros, from ancient **Eleutherna** (630-620 BC).
Poros models of birds set on a base with spiral decoration. The hawk was the sacred bird of Hera and the eagle that of Zeus. They come from the **sanctuary of Zeus Thenatas at Amnisos.**
Terracotta seated lion from **Praisos**, early 6th c. BC.
Archaic grave reliefs from the **cemeteries at Prinias**, one depicting a figure seated on a throne and the other a standing figure, probably a goddess, holding a wreath and a bird in her hands.
Terracotta base of a cylindrical statue from **Kavousi Ierapetras.**

East side
Large relief pithoi with scenes of cockerels, bulls and horses, from **Phaistos.**
Clay conical object decorated with lion's heads, possibly an altar cover, from the **acropolis at Gortyn.**

East wall (upper level)
Terracotta sima (waterspout) from the **temple of Diktaean Zeus at Palaikastro**, 6th c. BC. It depicts war chariots with charioteers and men armed with shields, helmets and lances. Dogs run alongside the chariots.

South side
Large piece of a marble kouros (statue of a naked male) from the **temple of Pythian Apollo at Gortyn.**
Pithos with relief scenes from **Lithines Siteias.**
Small poros head from **Axos.**
Stele with a scene of a winged figure, possibly Talos, and a gorgoneion, from **Dreros.**
Stele of black stone, on which is inscribed the famous **hymn to Zeus**. It comes from the **sanctuary of Diktaean Zeus at Palaikastro**. The inscription is carved on both sides of the

stone. The text contains an invocation to the "great Kouros" Zeus. who is invited to attend the festival held in his honour and fructify the fields and flocks.

Grave stele of the early 5th c. BC from **Kounavi** (ancient Eltyna) near Herakleion.

Archaic relief (650 BC) of a seated goddess from **Malles Ierapetras.**

The upper part of a larger than life size poros statue, of a seated figure, from **Astritsi.**

Centre of the room

Case 210

The trinity of gods from the Delphinion, the **temple of Apollo at Dreros**. These three superb bronze statues were made of hammered sheets of bronze nailed to a wooden core. They depict Apollo, on a larger scale than the other two gods, Artemis and Leto, and date from before 650 BC.

Cases 208, 209

Votive shields, bowls and cymbals from the **Idaean Cave**, in which Zeus was reared. According to tradition the Kouretes clashed their cymbals and shields together so that the noise would cover the crying of the infant god and prevent his father Kronos from hearing.

This scene is depicted on one of the cymbals in case 209. In the centre Zeus stands on a bull and tears a lion apart with his hands. Either side of him the Kouretes, shown as winged Assyrian daemons, clash four cymbals.

The shields have bosses in the shape of a lion's head and an eagle's head at the centre, and repoussé depictions of the Mistress of the Animals, shown naked amongst lions, as well as scenes of contests between humans and lions, sphinxes, snakes, etc.

One bowl has a depiction of women dancing and birds and fish being offered to the deity. Other bowls simply have rows of bulls, deer and other animals.

These objects date from c. 700 BC and reveal clear eastern influence, especially in the case of the large shields.

Three bronze hammered statues from Dreros. Apollo is in the centre, with Leto at the left and Artemis at the right.

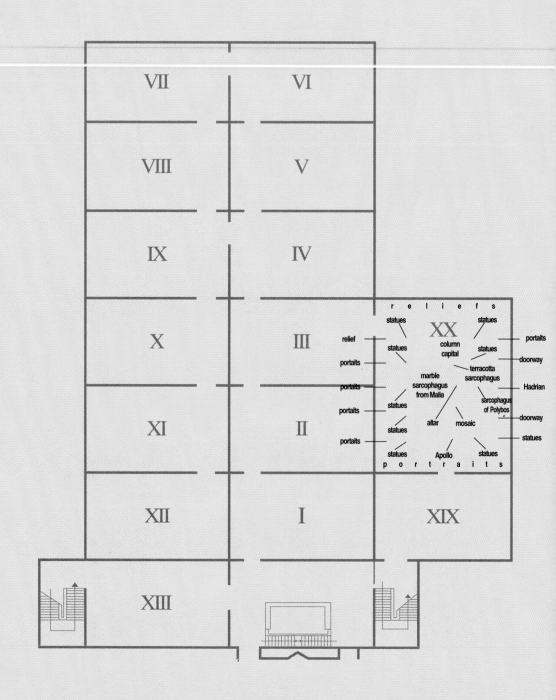

VII

VI

VIII

V

IX

IV

X

III

XI

II

XII

I

XIX

XIII

r e l i e f s

statues · statues

XX

column capital

statues · statues

relief

portaits

portaits

portaits

portaits

terracotta sarcophagus

marble sarcophagus from Malia

statues

statues

altar · mosaic

statues

Apollo · statues

p o r t r a i t s

portraits

doorway

Hadrian

sarcophagus of Polybos

doorway

statues

ROOM XX

CLASSICAL, HELLENISTIC AND GRECO-ROMAN SCULPTURE

T he finds in this room include: Classical grave stelai; a colossal statue of Apollo; copies of works by Poly-kleitos, Skopas, Alkamenes and Doidalsas; portraits of Roman emperors and nobles; a statue of Hadrian; statues of Serapis, Isis and Kerberos; statue of a philosopher; the Niobids; a Roman lady; a kore; a naked athlete; Zeus, Dionysos, Aphrodite and others.

Also on display is a mosaic with a depiction of Poseidon and his retinue; a marble relief sarcophagus; and the sarcophagus of Polybos.

The sculpture display in the Herakleion Museum comprises mainly works of Greco-Roman times, when Crete was a Roman province. Many of the sculptures of Roman date (1st-3rd c. AD) are copies of originals dating from the Classical period. The original sculptures of Classical and Hellenistic date (5th-1st c. BC), though few in number, are highly interesting. The sculptures come from all parts of the island, though mainly from the capital, **Gortyn, Knossos, Chersonisos, Lyttos, Ierapetra, Ayia Pelayia** (ancient **Apollonia**), ancient **Herakleion**, **Kissamos, Malia, Inatos, Lassia, Plora** (ancient **Pyloros**), **Lappa** (**Argyroupolis**) and other sites.

The sculptures have been divided into groups. Those from Gortyn are displayed on the north side of the room, those from Knossos and Archanes on the west, and those from Chersonisos, Malia, Kissamos, Lyttos and Ierapetra on the east. In the centre of the room is a mosaic floor from Knossos. Our visit begins on the south side of the room, to the left of the entrance, continues on the west side, followed by the north and east sides and the south side to the right of the entrance.

Headless marble statue of the emperor Hadrian, from Knossos.

South side
West of the entrance

Relief with the goddess Demeter mourning for the abduction of her daughter Persephone by Pluto, from **Knossos**, 1st-3rd c. AD **(15)**.

Decorative relief depicting Zeus/swan with Leda. Copy of a famous Classical work, from a private house at **Knossos**, 1st-2nd c. AD **(367)**.

Decorative relief depicting the struggle between Eros and Anteros. from a private house at **Knossos**, 1st-3rd c. AD **(368)**.

Two Erotideis fast asleep, from a child's tomb at **Knossos**, 1st-3rd c. AD **(281, 369)**

Small relief stele from **Lassaia** with the inscription (*GREETINGS YE THAT PASS BY I LEAVE MY FRIENDS BEHIND*). 3rd c. AD **(276)**.

Grave stele with the inscription *SOPHONOS SON OF MELANTHOS*.

Grave stele revealing Attic influence, showing the relatives and friends of a dead girl bidding her farewell. The girl sits with her feet resting on a footstool, while the standing child holds out its arms to her. The stele comes from **Lassaia** and dates from the late 5th c. BC **(471)**.

Two small altars from **Arkades** and **Knossos**, 1st-3rd c. AD **(246, 54)**.

Part of a child sarcophagus with relief decoration of Erotes, from **Gortyn**, 1st-3rd c. AD **(164)**.

Grave relief with a funeral banquet from ancient **Herakleion**. A couple is depicted on a couch with carved legs, and a second woman is shown on another couch. In front of the figures and couches can be seen two low tables with offerings. Three young servant girls approach carrying pyxides in their hands. Inscriptions record the names (*GOOD LAIS, DAUGHTER OF EUARESTOS FAREWELL*) and (*MARIA, GOOD TO ALL, FAREWELL*). The relief dates from the 3rd c. AD **(480)**.

Grave relief with a scene of five figures in a ship, from **Tymbaki**, 1st-3rd c. AD **(1112)**.

Grave stele of a horseman, of unknown provenance, 1st-3rd c. AD **(360)**.

Votive relief with the Dioskouroi, from **Knossos**, 1st-3rd c. AD **(17)**.

West side of the room, from the south
In front of the first pedestal

Headless statue of a youth wearing a *boulla* and holding a dove, from **Knossos**, 1st-3rd c. AD **(273)**.

Marble statue of a philosopher, from Gortyn.

On the first pedestal
Head of a woman with melon-shaped coiffure, from **Archanes**, 2nd c. AD **(211)**.
Copy dating from Roman times of the statue of Aphrodite of Knidos, from **Knossos**, 1st-3rd c. AD **(342)**.

On the second pedestal
Bust of a man from the family of Augustus, from **Knossos**, 1st-3rd c. AD **(503)**.

Between the two pedestals
Headless statue of a lady, possibly an empress, wearing a himation, from **Knossos**, 1st-3rd c. AD **(316)**.
Statuette of Dionysos crowned with ivy, from **Knossos**, 1st-3rd c. AD **(315)**.

On the third pedestal
Portal of a wealthy house with preserved coloured decoration, from **Knossos**, 3rd-1st c. BC (no number).

In front of the first pillar
Naked statue of a handsome youth from **Chersonisos**, 1st c. AD (no number).
Colossal statue of the emperor Hadrian, with the typical panoply worn by him, depicting deified Rome between figures of winged Victory standing on defeated foes. Rome stands on the wolf that suckled Romulus and Remus. The statue comes from **Knossos** and dates from the 2nd c. AD **(5)**.

Centre of the room
Marble sarcophagus with the inscription *POLYBOS* and relief scenes depicting a human skeleton, a *paidagogos* (tutor) with a cylindrical scroll in his hand, making a speech, and a flute-player. It also has scene of an offering-table with legs in the form of lions, bearing fruit and a kiste – the vessel associated with the Eleusinian mysteries, into which the dead man had possibly been initiated. It comes from **ancient Herakleion**, where it had been used as a basin in a fountain, as is clear from the holes. It dates from the 1st-3rd c. AD.
Mosaic floor made of small black and white tesserae forming decorative motifs and enclosing a depiction of the god Poseidon with his trident, riding on sea-horses. It is signed by the artist in Greek: *MADE BY APOLLINARIS*. It comes from a luxury residence at Knossos and dates from the 2nd c. AD.

Marble statue of the god
Dionysos, from Knossos.

Grave stele in the shape of an altar with the inscription *ACHIL-LES SON OF ACHILLES* and a scene of a man near a horse, and dogs chasing deer.

North side of the room, from the west
Torso of a naked youth, copy of the 5th c. BC Doryphoros (Spear-bearer) by Polykleitos, from **Gortyn**, 1st-3rd c. AD **(342)**.
Statue of Pothos (Desire), copy of a 4th c. BC original by Skopas, from **Gortyn**, 1st-3rd c. AD **(3)**.
Statue of Aphrodite in the Gardens, copy of a Classical work by Alkamenes in the 5th c. BC, from **Gortyn**, 1st-3rd c. AD **(325)**.
Statue of Aphrodite, copy of a Classical work by Praxiteles in the 4th c. BC, from **Gortyn**, 1st-3rd c. AD **(159)**.
Statue of Zeus abducting Ganymede, copy of a known Classical work, from **Gortyn**, 1st-3rd c. AD **(11)**.
Statue of Aphrodite, copy of a known Classical work by Doidalsas, from **Gortyn**, 1st-3rd c. AD **(43)**.

Around the north pillar
Statue of the god Apollo as a child, from the sanctuary of Asklepios at **Lebena** (modern Lenda), 1st-3rd c. AD **(146)**.
Statue of the goddess Athena Parthenos, copy of the Classical work by Pheidias, from **Gortyn**, 2nd c. AD **(347)**.

On the first pedestal
Five heads of statues of members of the family of the emperor Augustus, from **Gortyn**, 1st c. AD **(67, 65, 64, 66, 4)**.
Statues of the gods Pluto and Persephone with the figures of the Egyptian gods Serapis and Isis, from their temple at **Gortyn**, 1st-3rd c. AD **(259, 260)**.
Statue of the goddess Aphrodite with a bowl, from the **Nymphaion at Gortyn**, 1st-3rd c. AD **(154)**.
Colossal statue of the god Apollo, from the **temple of Pythian Apollo at Gortyn**, 1st-3rd c. AD **(326)**.
Statue of the god Pan, from **Gortyn**, 1st-3rd c. AD **(153)**.

On the third pedestal from the left
Portrait of a Cretan official or kosmos from **Gortyn**, 1st-3rd c. AD **(36)**.
Portraits of Roman emperors from **Gortyn**, 1st-3rd c. AD **(73, 60)**.
Statue of a philosopher with a staff and books, from Gortyn, 1st-3rd c. AD **(1)**.
Statue of the goddess Artemis in the Fields, copy of a Classical original, 1st-3rd c. AD **(208)**.

Marble statue of the goddess
Aphrodite holding a bowl,
from Gortyn.

Marble grave relief of a youth, from Ayia Pelayia.

Next to the north pillar

Half-naked statue of the goddess Aphrodite from Gortyn, 1st-3rd c. AD **(349).**

On the pedestal in the north-east corner

Bust of the god Dionysos, shown with horns, wearing an ivy wreath and pine-cones, and a panther skin on his breast. The statue base is in the form of a calyx. The bust comes from **Plora in Mesara** and dates from the 2nd c. AD (470).

East side of the room
On the first pedestal behind the Niobids.

Bust of the emperor Marcus Aurelius **(230)**, head of the emperor Trajan **(317),** head of a lady **(389)** and head of a eunuch **(344)**, from Lyttos, 1st-3rd c. AD.

On round pedestals

Three headless and incomplete female statues from Lyttos. The two with the snake symbol are possibly of the goddess Hygeia, 1st-3rd c. AD **(312, 335, 313).**

In front of the first pedestal

Statue of a kore. copy of an early 5th c. BC original. This statue reveals the tendency on the part of some artists in the Roman period to imitate Archaic originals. The sparse, severe drapery, which recalls a Doric column, is characteristic. The neck, head and arms were made from a separate piece of marble and have not been preserved. It comes from ancient Kissamos and dates from the 1st-3rd c. AD **(2).**

In front of the second pedestal

Statue of a woman, possibly an empress, wearing a long peplos and himation that also covers her head, with its characteristic coiffure. From Chersonisos, 2nd c. AD **(334).**
Statue of the god Pan holding the pipes (syrinx) in his right hand, close to his mouth; he holds a sheep with his left hand and wears a sheepskin. The statue comes from **Argyroupolis** (ancient **Lappa**) and dates from the 1st-3rd c. AD **(472).**
The goddess Artemis wearing hunting boots (endromides) shoots an arrow at one of the Niobids, while her mother Niobe tries to shield her with her body. Copy of a known 4th c. BC original multifigural composition from **Inatos**, 1st-3rd c. AD **(265, 266).**
Large intact Attic sarcophagus of Pentelic marble with relief

Marble relief slab with a chariot drawn by two lions and driven by a child.

scenes depicting winged Erotideis, heads of Medusa, bucrania, lion's heads, lions, eagles, and wreaths and guilloches of leaves and fruit. The gold jewellery found in the sarcophagus is displayed in Room XVIII, case 207. The sarcophagus was found beneath the altar of the Early Christian basilica at **Marmara Malion**, which dates from the 6th c. AD. The sarcophagus was made in the 2nd c. AD and was reused in the 3rd or 4th c. to bury a man and a woman **(367)**.

On the fourth pedestal
Three heads of statues, the first two being copies of originals dating from the Classical period, from **Ierapetra**, 1st-3rd c. AD **(76, 75, 148)**.
Head of a male statue depicting an African, from Bengazi, 1st-3rd c. AD **(50)**.

Around the south pillar
Hermaic stele from west Crete, dating from Roman times (25).

Headless statue of a half-naked man from **Chersonisos**, 1st-3rd c. AD **(467)**.

South side of the room
To the right of the entrance
Grave stele in the shape of a small temple with a scene of relatives bidding farewell to the deceased, from **Herakleion**, 4th c. BC **(378)**.
Poros metope from a temple, depicting Herakles and the Erymanthian boar, from **Knossos**, 5th c. BC **(363)**.
Grave stele of a young huntsman from **Ayia Pelayia** near **Herakleion**, early 4th c., BC **(145)**.
Part of a relief sarcophagus with a scene of the hunt for the Calydonian boar, from **Chersonisos**, 2nd-3rd c. AD **(249)**.
Part of a relief sarcophagus depicting Bellerophon with the winged Pegasos **(9)**.
Part of a relief sarcophagus with a scene of warfare **(12)**.

Poros relief metope showing Herakles and the Erymanthean boar, from Knossos.

O ur visit to the part of the Herakleion Archaeological Museum open to the public comes to an end at this point. Visitors who wish to see and study other finds that are not on display should notify the appropriate Museum service in good time for their request to be considered and for assistance to be offered.

The Archaeological Museum also includes the Epigraphic Collection which is housed in the bastion in the fortifications to the south of and opposite the Museum. Prior notification is also needed to visit this Collection.

This first acquaintance with the monuments of Cretan civilisation in the Archaeological Museum should, of course, be extended by a visit to the Historical Museum of Crete, which is housed in the Kalokerinos villa next to the Xenia Hotel in Herakleion. This museum has an exemplary display of objects illustrating the civilisation of Crete from the Early Byzantine period (4thc. AD) to the middle of the 20th century.

Visitors should also not fail to visit the major archaeological sites of Crete at which the monuments housed in the Museum were found, in order to form as complete a possible a picture of the Cretan civilisation.

The Minoan palace towns at Knossos, Phaistos, Malia, Zakros, Ayia

Triada, Archanes, Monastiraki, Galatas and Petra. The Minoan towns and settlements at Kommos, Palaikastro, Gournia, Tylissos, Mochlos, Pseira, Vasiliki, Apodoulou, Zominthos, Chondros, Myrtos and Trypiti. The Minoan megara and villas at Nirou, Amnisos, Chamaizi, Gortyn, Vathypetro, Siteia, Nerokourou, Makriyalo and elsewhere.

The cult caves: the Idaean Cave, Diktaean Cave, the cave of Kamares, the caves of Eileithyia at Amnisos and Inatos, the cave of Skoteinos, the cave of Hermes Krannaios at Patsos, the caves of Melidoni, Mamelouko, Yerani and the sanctuaries on Mount Juktas and at Symi.

The Minoan cemeteries at Phourni, Archanes, at Armeni, Ayia Photia, Koumasa, at the Odigitria Monastery at Platanos, and at Lenda.

The settlements-refuges of the Protogeometric period at Vrokastro, Kavousi, Vigla Pigaidakion and Karphi.

The cities of the Archaic period at Prinias, Dreros, Lato, Praisos and Goudeliana.

The cities that flourished in the Roman and Early Byzantine periods, the capital Gortyn, Chersonisos, Hierapytna, Lyttos, Itanos, Phalasarna, Eleutherna, Axos, Sybritos, Lappa, Aptera, Lissos, Elyros, Syia and Halmyris.

The Epigraphic Collection building.

A

abacus
Rectangular slab forming the upper part of a column-capital.

alabaster
Kind of yellowish white gypsum.

alabastron
Vase with a round base and piriform or squat body.

alternating style
Vase-painting style of the late New Palace period (1500-1450 BC), in which decorative elements are repeated over the entire surface of the vase.

anaklintron
Bed with a head support.

apotropaic
Having magical powers to ward off evil.

argonaut
See nautilus argonaut.

Arimaspaeans
A mythical people that lived in the north of Scythia and had only one eye, like the Cyclopes. They were in a permanent state of war with the Griffins (q.v.).

aryballos
Vase with a globular body, low neck, flat rim and two handles. Used for perfume or aromatic oil.

astragal
Moulding with a curved profile.

Ayios Onouphrios style
Vase-painting style of the early Pre-palace period (3500-2800 BC), with dark linear decoration on a light surface.

azurite
A material with a deep blue colour, imported from Egypt and used in wall-paintings.

B

barbotine style
Vase-painting style of the late Pre-palace and early Old Palace period (2100-1800 BC), in which the vases have relief surfaces, occasionally painted.

boar's tusk helmet
leather helmet covered with boar's tusks.

brazier
shallow clay vase with a horizontal handle, used for carrying burning coals.

bronze talent
Quadrilateral piece of bronze with slightly incurving sides; ingot; unit of the mass of the metal.

bucranium
Likeness of a bull's skull.

bull-leaping
Acrobatic sport in which the acrobats leap over a bull, an act of initiation.

C

cartouche
(Egyptian archaeology) oval border with a straight line at one end, containing the hieroglyphic rendering of a royal name.

chlorite
Mineral of a greenish colour. Used to make stone vases or vessels.

codpiece
Type of loincloth (q.v.) covering only the pudenda.

communion chalice
Vase with a tall stem, used in rituals.

confronted
(Figures) set facing each other.

conglomerate
Type of volcanic rock (andesite) of a green colour. Used for decorative purposes and for works of art.

coroplasty
The manufacture of terracotta figurines (q.v.).

cutout
In metalworking, pieces (usually small plaques or jewellery) shaped and cut from a large sheet of metal.

D

dagger
Small knife used as a weapon. Small sword.

deposit
Pit containing a large number of finds, either dedications or waste objects.

dinos
Large vase with a globular body, usually supported on a stand, used to mix wine.

E

earring
Item of jewellery worn in the ear.

eggshell vase
Category of Kamares style (q.v.) vase with very thin walls.

Ephyrean kylix style
Vase-painting style of the Creto-Mycenaean period (1450-1350 BC), in which the basic shape is the deep two-handled cup with a tall stem, decorated with one motif on each side of the surface.

erotideis
Depictions of the young Eros, used as decorative motifs.

F

faience
Mixture of sand, quartz, soda and lime, covered with polish. Used in figurines and jewellery. It has a black, dark blue, greenish-blue or off-white colour.

fibula
Metal ornament used for fastening clothing, kind of safety-pin.

figurine
Small model in clay, stone, metal or other material, with a naturalistic or stylised rendering of a human or animal. Small statue.

floral style
Vase-painting style of the New Palace period (1650-1450 BC), in which the vases are decorated with floral and vegetal motifs in a dark colour on a light background.

frieze
1. The central part of the entablature above the architrave, usually decorated with a multi-figural sculptured or painted scene.
2. (Minoan archaeology) part of the wall-painted decoration of the surface of a wall with a multi-figural scene.

fruit-stand
Vase shape with a high foot, probably used for holding fruit.

funerary
That which is placed as a marker (statue, vase, slab, stele etc.) above a grave or tumulus.

G

girdle
Piece of armour worn by Cretans around the waist, beneath the breastplate, to protect the belly.

glass paste
(Minoan and Mycenaean) the earliest form of glass, a blend of quartz, gypsum and soda. Used to make beads, plaques, amulets and inlays. Usually of a blue, bluish-grey, white or yellow colour.

gorgoneion
Terrifying mask of the Gorgon's head, with fierce eyes, sharp teeth and a merciless gaze. It had an apotropaic (q.v.) character.

granulation
Form of decoration of gold jewellery in which tiny granules of gold are attached to the metal surface, creating a variety of decorative motifs.

grave offerings
Offerings to the dead placed in graves or burnt along with the body. They consisted of jewellery and other favourite items of the dead person.

griffin
Imaginary winged beast, a combination of lion and eagle. The griffins have been placed variously in Scythia, near the legendary Arimaspaeans (q.v.), in the East, or in India.
From the East they entered Minoan and later Archaic Greek art.

H

hammered
Made from a piece of metal hammered by a suitable tool; relief.

Hamurabi
King of Mesopotamia in the second half of the 18th c. BC.

horns of consecration
Minoan religious symbol imitating bull's horns. Used to decorate the cornice of Minoan buildings and as a decorative motif in wall- and vase-painting.

I

ideogram
Sign or symbol of a script that represents an idea rather than a phoneme or a syllable. The earliest of the three writing systems of Minoan Crete was an ideogrammatic script.

ithyphallic
With the male member erect.

J

jug
Vase shape with a single handle, piriform body, neck and spout usually in the shape of a bird's beak.

K

kalpe
Large vase used to draw water, a type of pitcher. Also used as a cinerary urn to contain the ashes of a dead person.

Kamares style
Vase-painting style of the Old Palace period (1900-1500 BC), in which the vases have polychrome decoration of linear and other motifs executed in white and red on a black burnished surface.

kantharos
Vase shape with a deep cavity, and two vertical handles that project from the rim and end low on the belly. Used for drinking wine, and the favourite vase of Dionysos.

kernos
1. Clay rhyton consisting of several vases of the same type.
2. Stone cult vessel with several cavities, used for offerings of seeds, fruit or liquids.

kiste
Type of box used in mystery rituals (e.g. the Eleusinian mysteries).

Koumasa style
Vase-painting style of the middle Pre-palace period (2800-2300 BC), a development of the Ayios Onouphrios style, with stylised linear motifs.

Kouretes
Mythical daemons who reared the infant Zeus in Crete.

kourotrophos
Type of figurine with a female figure holding the divine infant in her hands.

krater
Large vase with a bulky body and wide mouth, used for mixing wine with water.

L

larnax
See sarcophagus.

libation vase
Category of vase used for liquid offerings (libations).

lime-plaster
Plaster made with lime, water and grains of sand, pumice or marble, which was highly durable when it dried.

Linear A script
Writing system used in the New Palace period (1700-1450 BC) to record lists of goods and produce incised on clay tablets, and also for prayers on cult objects. The language of the tablets has not yet been deciphered, though it may have been an early form of Greek (Indo-European).

Linear B script
Writing system used at Knossos and Kydonia

and also on the Greek mainland during the Creto-Mycenaean period (1450-1200 BC) to record lists of goods and produce, written on incised tablets. The language of the tablets was Mycenaean Greek.

loincloth
Short garment worn by men skirt to cover the pudenda and part of the thighs.

lopada
Shallow bowl.

M

marine style
Vase-painting style of the New Palace period (1650-1450 BC), in which the vases are decorated with motifs drawn from the world of the sea, executed in a dark colour on a light background.

megaron
(Minoan archaeology) large two-storey building imitating the architecture of the palaces; wealthy residence, seat of a local governor.

microlithic tools
Small stone tools, usually of obsidian or quartz.

miniature scenes
Scenes in which the figures are of small dimensions.

mistress of the animals
Female deity, protectress of wild animals, later identified with Artemis.

N

nautilus argonaut
Marine mollusc of the cephalopod class, with tentacles in its mouth that it uses to seize its food. Common in Minoan art as a decorative motif (see marine style).

O

obsidian
Type of volcanic rock of a black, shiny appearance. Used to make microlithic tools (q.v.) and, more rarely, vases.

offering-table
Cult vessel used as an altar; it was circular with three feet, or stepped and inverted, and was made of terracotta, gypsum plaster or stone.

oinochoe
Vase with a handle and trefoil or round mouth, commonly used for pouring wine.

Orientalising style
Vase-painting style of the 7th century BC, in which the vases are decorated with motifs and representations drawn from the Orient (griffins, sphinxes, lions, etc.).

oryctes nasicornis
Kind of beetle with a horn on its head. Models of it were placed as dedications in peak sanctuaries.

P

palace style
Vase-painting style of the period 1450-1350 BC, characterised mainly by the use of stylised decorative motifs.

palmette
Floral ornament based on the leaf of a palm-tree.

peak sanctuary
Cult place on a mountain top, enclosed within a low wall and with an altar at the centre, on which votive offerings were placed.
They were exclusively and characteristically associated with Minoan religion, and flourished mainly in the Old Palace period.

pin
Ornament in the shape of a pin used to fasten clothing or decorate the hair.

pithamphoreas
Large vase shape, a pithos with three or more handles at the shoulder.

polos
Cylindrical head-cover.

portal
Large outer doorway that served as the main entrance to a palace, megaron, temple, etc.

prochoidio
Small jug.

Pyrgos style
Pottery style of the early Pre-palace period (3500-2800 BC), in which the vases have a grey or black burnished surface.

pyxis
Vase with a cylindrical or spherical body and lid. Used as a jewellery box.

R

---

repoussé
Relief ornamentation executed in metal by striking it from the reverse side.

revetment
The covering of the lower part of walls with slabs of marble or gypsum.

rhyton
Vessel or vase, usually with one handle, used for liquid offerings (libations). It normally has a hole in the bottom. Some were in the shape of humans or animals.

rock crystal
Type of translucent semiprecious stone. Used to make small works of art.

Roman colony
The political regime imposed by the Romans at Knossos, which resisted the Roman conquest. Knossos was not allowed local self-government, like other cities, but was ruled by a Roman governor. Roman colonists were also settled there.

S

---

sacral knot
Minoan religious symbol with a magical purpose, consisting of a strip of coloured material with fringes, a ring in the centre, and the two ends hanging free, like a modern tie.

sarcophagus (also larnax)
Coffin: a terracotta, stone or marble oval, bathtub- or cist-shaped vessel used for burials.

scarab
The scarab beetle, a member of the order of coleoptera, of which the sub-species the sacred scarab was thought to symbolise the sun and was worshipped by the Egyptians.
Models of scarabs were inscribed with hieroglyphic inscriptions.

sealing
Imprint of a seal made on a piece of clay while soft.

serpentine
Soft stone of dark green, brown or black colour, used to make stone vases and jewellery.

sherd
Small fragment of a ceramic vase. Also potsherd.

sistrum
Rattle: a musical instrument with a metal, clay or wooden frame shaped like a horseshoe, with small vertical rods on which discs are threaded that produce a sound when the instrument is moved rhythmically.

skyphos
Deep vase with two handles and a wide mouth.

sphinx
Mythical beast with the body of a lion and head of a woman.

spindlewhorl
Small round object pierced with a hole, used to steady the spindle when carding wool.

stand
Support, foot or base for vases with globular bodies (e.g. cauldrons).

steatite
Soft stone of a grey-green colour. Used to make sealstones and other works of art.

steatopygous
Describes a type of female figurine in which the buttocks and thighs are exaggerated.

stirrup jar
Vase with two handles and two necks, one of which is a false mouth.

sword pommel
Handle of a sword or dagger, in the shape of a mushroom.

T

---

tablet
(Minoan archaeology) a piece of clay in the shape of a rectangular "page", incised with Linear A or Linear B inscriptions.

trickle decoration
Decorative technique used mainly in large Mi-noan vases, in which the colour was applied freely in large drops or "trickles".

tripartite shrine
The main shrine at Knossos. The central section, which had a single column, was higher than the two wings at the side, which had two columns each. (The miniature fresco shows a different arrangement of columns.)

V

Vasiliki style
Vase-painting style of the middle Pre-palace period (2800-2300 BC), in which the vases have a mottled surface caused by uneven firing.

villa
(Minoan archaeology) large, well-built and lavishly decorated house in the countryside that belonged to a local governor, official or wealthy individual.

votive
Object dedicated to the gods.

W

---

wedding cauldron
Large vase with a globular body, cylindrical, flat rim, and two double handles, that rested on a stand. Presented as a gift to the bride.

white style
Vase-painting style of the late Pre-palace period (2300-1900 BC), in which the vases are decorated with linear motifs executed in white paint on a dark ground.